Suffer
the Children

Critical praise for
Djelloul Marbrook's fiction

Guest Boy, Book 1 Light Piercing Water trilogy
(2018, Leaky Boot Press)

What Marbrook does so well in *Guest Boy* is the contradictory elegance
he showed in *Saraceno*. He finds the tender and poetic heart of very tough
men. In *Saraceno*, it was low-level mobsters; in *Guest Boy*, it's men of the
sea. They're a horny-handed bunch, and Marbrook's familiarity with
ships and the characters of mean-street ports is deep and exciting. But
Marbrook knows that these guys have a lot more going on within, and
are simultaneously deeply tender philosophers. It's a mesmerizing book...
You'll find yourself thinking about it long after you've finished reading.

—Dan Baum, author of *Gun Guys* (2013), *Nine Lives* (2009), and others

Guest Boy is a complex work: deep, passionate, exciting and beautifully
written with flashbacks and imagery merging real and surreal. By opening
up routes to the culture and history of the Arab world, *Guest Boy* helps us
understand that world and our own.

—Sanford Fraser, author of *Tourist* and *Among Strangers I've Known All My Life*

... it is in books like this that I seek answers and guidance as I travel my
own path to enlightenment and contentment. This book opened a struggle
in me...

—Isla McKetta, editor, *A Geography of Reading*

Artemisia's Wolf
(title story, *A Warding Circle*, 2017, Leaky Boot Press)

... Djelloul Marbrook's impressive novella ... successfully blends humor and
satire (and perhaps even a touch of magic realism) into its short length ... an
engrossing story, but what might strike the reader most throughout the book
is its infusion of breathtaking poetry ... a stunning rebuke to notoriously
misogynist subcultures like the New York art scene, showing us just how
hard it is for a young woman to be judged on her creative talent alone.

—Tommy Zurhellen, *Hudson River Valley Review*

... lets his powerful imagination run wild, leading the fiction into unexpected
corners where weird performers hold court and produce endings that both astonish
and are frequently magical.

—James Polk, *The Country and Abroad*, former contributing editor of *Art/World*.

Saraceno

Djelloul Marbrook writes dialogue that not only entertains with an
intoxicating clickety-clack, but also packs a truth about low-life mob
culture "The Sopranos" only hints at. You can practically smell the anisette
and filling-station coffee.

—Dan Baum, author of *Gun Guys* (2013), *Nine Lives: Mystery,
Magic, Death and Life in New Orleans* (2009), and others

...a good ear for crackling dialogue ... I love Marbrook's crude, raw music of the streets. The notes are authentic and on target ...

—Sam Coale, *The Providence* (RI) *Journal*

... an entirely new variety of gangster tale ... a Mafia story sculpted with the most refined of sensibilities from the clay of high art and philosophy . .. the kind of writer I take real pleasure in discovering ... a mature artist whose rich body of work is finally coming to light.

—Brent Robison, editor, *Prima Materia*

Alice Miller's Room
(title story, *Making Room*, 2017, Leaky Boot Press)

This enchanting novella is a delicately wrought homage to Jung's famous principle of meaningful coincidence...

—*Breakfast All Day*, UK

... the story draws us into that mysterious and terrifying realm where the heart will have its say and all who enter leave transformed...

—Dr. Patricia L. Divine, Head Start program lifetime service award winner

Mean Bastards Making Nice (2014, Leaky Boot Press)

I love it. I admire it. It is you at your best.

—Best-selling novelist Gail Godwin, on "The Pain of Wearing Our Faces"

☙

Critical praise for
Djelloul Marbrook's poetry

Far from Algiers (2008, Kent State University Press)

... as succinct as most stanzas by Dickinson... an unusually mature, confidently composed first poetry collection.

—Susanna Roxman, *Prairie Schooner*
(author of *Crossing the North Sea*)

... brings together the energy of a young poet with the wisdom of long experience.

—Edward Hirsch, Guggenheim Foundation

... honors a lifetime of hidden achievement.

—Toi Derricotte, Wick Award judge

... wise and flinty poems outfox the furies of exile, prejudice, and longing... a remarkable and distinctive debut.

—Cyrus Cassells, National Poetry Series winner

Brash Ice (2014, Leaky Boot Press)

... resonates with wisdom and a keen eye for the beautiful things of this world ... a poetry that would make brash ice melt again.

—George Drew, author of *The View From Jackass Hill*

... a precision that occasionally recalls Yeats ...

—James Polk, *The Country and Abroad*

... aesthetically pleasing, thematically intriguing ...

—Michael Young, *The Poetry*

Brushstrokes and glances (2010, Deerbrook Editions)

Whether it is commentary on state power, corporate greed, or the intensely personal death of a loved one, Djelloul Marbrook is clear sighted, eloquent, and precise. As the title of the collection suggests, he uses the lightest touch, a collection of fragments, brushstrokes and glances, to fashion poems that resonate with truth and honesty.

—Phil Constable, *New York Journal of Books*

... looks at art the way a drinker drinks—deeply, passionately, and desperately, as if his life depended on it ... makes you want to run out to your favorite museum and look again, as you have never looked before, until the lights go out.

—Barbara Louise Ungar, author of *Thrift*; *Charlotte Bronte, You Ruined My Life*; *The Origin of the Milky Way*

... one of those colossal poets able to bridge worlds—poetry and art, heart and mind—with rare wit, grace, and sincerity; a soft-spoken artist with the courage to face the "fatal beckoning" of his muse ... crisp intellect, seamlessly interwoven with loss and longing. ... poetry at its best: at once both gritty and refined, private and political, tender and tough as iron ... well worth reading."

—Michael Meyerhofer, author of *What to do if you're buried alive*, *Damnatio Memoriae*, *Blue Collar Eulogies*

...delicately wrought... highly recommended reading...because, ultimately, this witness so clearly loves his subject.

—Eileen Tabios, Editor, *Galatea Resurrects*

Riding Thermals to Winter Grounds (2017, Leaky Boot Press)

... some very powerful lines, such as: "And then, near the end of my life, I become the man I wanted to be without the fuss and bother of giving a damn."

—Sidney Grayling, editor, Onager Editions

I don't know anyone else whose writing increases in agility and breadth over time as his does.

—Lee Gould, editor, La Presa, the Embajadoro Press poetry journal

Suffer
the Children

Sailing Her Navel: Poems
& Ludilon: A short novel

Djelloul Marbrook

LEAKY BOOT PRESS

Suffer the Children
Sailing Her Navel: Poems & Ludilon: A short novel
by Djelloul Marbrook

Acknowledgments

"The suffocating room" appeared in *Onager Editions*, July 2016.
"When our parents were bothering us" and "Build a cello"
appeared in *Dove Tales 2016*, the *Writing for Peace* anthology, May 2016.
"Build a cello" also appeared in *Red Sky*, the Sable Books anthology
about violence against women, October 2016.
"Bail to crucifix" appeared in *La Presa*, the Embajadoras Press journal,
in the May–June 2017 issue.

ISBN: 978-1-909849-80-8

First published in 2019 by Leaky Boot Press
Copyright © 2019 Djelloul Marbrook

*We do not just fear our predators,
we are transfixed by them. We are
prone to weave stories and fables
and chat endlessly about them.*

—Peter Benchley

*There was something delightfully intimate
about the relationship between predator
and prey.*

—Nenia Campbell, *Horrorscape*

For Sally

Author's Acknowledgments

Endless thanks are owed to my wife, Marilyn, who has in so many ways made all my work possible; to James Goddard, my publisher, whose steadfast faith in my work brought it to light and buoyed me in rough waters; to Sebastien Doubinsky, who published my work and introduced me to James Goddard; to Brent Robison, whose wizardly videos and deft hand with e-books still astonish me; to Kevin Swanwick, whose radiance as a reader and advisor unfailingly enlightens me, and to Emily Brooks, whose artistic taste, good cheer and resourcefulness seem fathomless.

Contents

Sailing Her Navel

Poems

Contents

Growing up spent

Salt dismay

In me

Aisling's inlet

The most troubling angel

An old man, once called Pip, now called Bo, sets sail in a paper boat, this paper boat, on the roiling sea of a giantess's navel. He fears he won't return. On the first page of his rutter he writes, Here be dragons. He sails a sea of recollection—tears, trysts, frights, abuse—the liquid elements of alchemy and confabulation. The names of the people you hear have been changed, but he recalls what happened as best he can. They are Aisling Wynant, giantess by virtue of her crimes against Sally, the girl who unerringly utters the one thing everyone else is moving heaven and earth not to hear, and Pip, the silent berserker. The old man believes that to die without trying to navigate this uncharted sea would be his own crime. He can only imagine what Aisling and Sally would say, or how they might say it. This is his rutter, the way sailors described their voyages before there were charts.

Growing up spent

Do this in remembrance...

Nothing is intimate enough to thaw the fimbulwinter
in a ruined child's marrow, no setting kind enough,
no face innocent enough, but willow in the rain,
egrets taking flight, will sometimes assuage
the ghostly ache that wanders room to room
fingering trinkets, rotting memories
of questions turned to stutters
and answers withheld.

Nothing can shake loose the frozen words
that would have called to an accounting
the tall caretakers who looked away as if
the child were about to say the one thing
for which no language has a word, the one thing
which once heard unravels all that is agreed upon,
whereupon the planetary system of the mind
throws its axis on the mercy of black holes.

Pronouns trail off into private reveries,
but not you, no, the second person who
rolls onward like wheels, that person draws
the poison out of us—I, me, they and them—
and disappears around the corner leaving children
shivering in the street, unable to grow up, to come in
from the cold embrace to which nothing will ever compare.

Growing up spent

Some people complete a circuit,
others break or short it out.
Some people never learn to dance,
maybe they weren't loved enough
or seemed a kind of sooty receptacle.
Some people need too much repair,
burnt and needing to be replaced,
others are too inviting to risk,
amiss for having been tampered with.
It was too memorable. They grew up spent,
Sally and Pip, and no one would do
because they had done too much,
too much had been done them.
They feared to find each other
for fear they would have grown away,
so they were stuck and incomplete,
undone, unable to grow old,
children frozen in a molester's hands,
unapproachable, absent, lost.
Men in Sally's life are distinguished
by not being Pip, women
in his life by not being Sally,
and what they're not is a crime
any way you look at it, Aisling Wynant's crime,
but she's off scot-free, or is she?
They don't know. All they know is
she's long gone from the scene of the crime
and they are her crime, is what they know.

Sailing her navel

Words close-hauled in her navel.
Consonants spanking. Vowels ahoist.
This orgiastic being, stars her trigger points,
perspires us to help divine her ecstasies,
and we have yet to recover landing parties
sent out to explore her nether zones.
Her hard breathing capsizes
our grandest navies.

We're her wishes, whimsies, wantons,
but her desires elude us, and yet
we must fulfill them. Life, death,
all our notions are her inconveniences
if not her toiletries. She changes
her position to tryst beyond imaginings;
we call this weather and the names
of other paper boats. Here be dragons
and there the shadows of her tits.

Abandon hope. Survive
only to transfigure lee to weather helm,
hard over to oblivion, getting drunk
on her excretions. We're her antibodies and elixirs,
her examiners and ennoblers,
essential to her butterflies and bees,
her consciousness and introspection,
the currents of her circuitries,
her salvific hymn.

Never mind jet planes and other apparatuses,
we must banshee this
on winged memories of her vineyards—

the painted values
of our nostalgia long
for this derangement. Hoist the diacriticals,
signal the others to jettison
the belongings of raptor merchants.
We don't need to eat or work for them.
Jolly Roger gives us free pratique.

The ports we've marked are portals,
explaining why they seem not there.
Set foot
among her body hairs.
Fall down
the black holes of her pores.
Sing
glorias and aves.

Disappear.

Seven-foot perp

Distort the facts for heaven's sake if not your own,
it doesn't matter, life's a comet's tail. These rooms
can't be bleached or painted over, even if Abounding Grace
squats over them now, and no amount of piety or prayer
can undo what happened to Sally and Pip in this distillate mind
that holds its secrets inside my name and finally decides
no one is worthy of them, except perhaps the seven-foot perp,
and who knows what happened to her in Arizona turquoise,
denial and preoccupation with being right? Who knows
whether she exulted to the end? Does it ever end?
How can the flowers bear it as its reverberances pollinate
the sinuses of children born to ride red wagons down
local stops and out in front of the Coney Island express?

Salt dismay

Salt dismay

I am Pip. I can only imagine
what Sally or Aisling would say.
No third person here. We are one,
a nightmare marriage indivisible,
invisible to each other, wed
inextricably to each other.
No omniscient narrator here
to remark on this and that,
to digress the way molesters
and enablers do.
I am Pip, determined
to say this if it kills me, but beware:
I don't know how this alchemy
turns out or what its elixir is.
I stand here in this frozen park
among strangers, my life
two strangers' hands
on an icy wheel. I study them
as if they'd been my own,
for convenience's sake, but now
I can't go on pretending nothing happened
that could not be undone.
Nothing happens but what happens
to all of us. Is that true or is there
a greater truth in how unique
our responses are, how we raise
memory palaces of sheer pain
shot through with each other's light?
I'm looking straight at you, Aisling,

through salt dismay. My vowels
set sail on consonants, I heel over
from dragons' breath, my timbers
open letting your excrescences in,
my timbre may not hit that angel note
but you will recognize its eerie hymns.
My descenders, keel and rudder, dig
into your black sea's parting robes,
but not even my signals are flying
because I intend to give no clue
where and when I might bear down.

This is my rutter, all of this,
these grunts and gronks aspiring
to notes I had a hard time carrying
after you, after what I intend
to explore, lay out in grids, here
where dragons play and blow around
our paper ships on your orders.
You're tied like sacrifice to the stone
of recollection and can't put your
finger on this tiny ship in your navel,
can't scratch this itch as once you did
with us. All you can do is imagine
what we've become because of you,
what we made of it, made of you.
Straight at you, Aisling, with unblinking eye,
sailing chartless into the maelstrom
for one reason only, to rub out
the sob you put in me as surely
as you put me in you and Sally.

I am Pip, captain of this reckless odyssey,
looking straight at you, Aisling,
through salt dismay and memory stripped
of hemming, hawing and sucking up.
I am Pip, and that's what I intend,
to show that light if I can, to guess

what Sally/Pip/Aisling have become
and to assign to them a few words
that might strike someone as true.
I start with Sally than whom
no one else is like or even able
to remind me of her, Sally, the one
who never had to forgive me,
whom I never had to forgive, the one
I think of when my thinking's done
and nothing remains but exhaustion
blessed in its innocence. I speak here
in the voices that come to me
out of gibberish, salvage, debris fields
I've had to dive on to dredge up
the record of a frightful journey.

They don't survive the oxygen
and so you hear them dying
as they speak. Find respite then
in the few words I imagine
Sally and Aisling might speak,
respite—of solace there is none
but in the truth we three are one.

Watchful child

I crawl into bed knees first, like a child
or a soldier under a hail of tracers;
I don't trust the world to be there for my ass
nor do I sleep on my back where they can get me,
they being you and other ogres of the night,
nor can I sleep with my heart exposed;
my side sinister, bastard side, is what is left,
and there my right eye searches the terrain
for any dreams that might go over to the enemy
before I wake. I will die a watchful child.

Pip's corpses

Corpses of dreams bob up
from the bottom of the lake
where I anchored them—
my mother chopped to pieces
on hot Manhattan roofs,
me on an American Flyer hurtling
down subway steps—
corpses staring me in the face,
bloated, bitten, unbidden,
tripping my breaker box
with their cold hands,
home now to snakes writhing
among my engagements.

Lake of past lives, past lies,
grotesque creatures,
do I fish you consciously
or sleepwalk by your shores?

How can death be riddance
when I'm accustomed to it?

I fly along remembered esplanades,
recognizing neighborhoods
that belie my biography.
They're not as eager to be rid of me
as a pack of familiars are.

I've put my Tarot down and asked
the cruelest questions I could bear,
painted shame with Luminol
to study its blue light,

convincing evidence of crimes,
and yet I don't know whose.

Where is my birth certificate?
I'll never know, but I've learned
to respect bastardy.

Stormlight

We're termites and teredos
to our better selves, eating up
the vessels of our progress,
and when they founder we look
for islands of books to cower
under shades of ideas
we'd piss on in drier times.
We may not drown today
or tomorrow but soon enough
we'll navigate the glacier melt
to isles of arcana we deny
when we're high on gasoline
and fools' hoo-ha. Soon enough
we'll swim exudations of gods,
abjure our faith in politics,
predators' hoards, whorish devices.
But not now when pumps
still work and seacocks keep
our bilges dry. Not yet,
not ever if we can rise
above presumptions to
the green flash of inquiry.

Child waving

Pour pale sea glass into a carafe,
lodge it in a stream bed,
will it curse the mother river,
interrupt barge traffic
out of alien pique or
will it bless the six-hour tides

with a holy ghostliness
redolent of exquisite gesture,
gesture like a child waving
at a perfect stranger on a bus?
I don't know, but I do care
more than I care about politics

or even my past misdeeds,
more, I think, than tomorrow,
which might never come, not
in any case for me, care more
than any sails I've perfumed
to ply goddesses' navels.

What shut his current down

Drugs are tested better than what I had to measure
the jolts and griefs of my childhood,
and we know how well drugs are tested.
What shut my current down nests in my confabulations;
I've had enough of it to be immune
to fear if not clot and wilt,
and out of the sanctimonium of middle age I've shot
a bolt of uncaring in the face of myth so as not to leave behind
a pile of touted junk prettied up and sold as pricey salvage.
I know what grids I've strung out
at what depths, and I've brought up
what could survive the oxygen and light;
the rest I leave to sea beds heaving and hovering
and shadows overhead.

Bo to Pip

I

You don't remember green clouds lowering
or piping me to heaven in a squall.
I could see through red blindfolds
and not be made to turn away.
Your friends wept in their pillows for English homes.
They'd come to escape the Luftwaffe, but you
sent me home from the horrors of the camp.
Gods can save anyone but themselves
and that is why they have their stories.
Now your story's somewhat different.
You thought you called up that hell
by some ill omen in you and you saw
no reason I should suffer it.
How is it now you speak of my deserting,
speaking too cogently to be believed?
Why should the bastards have gotten two for one?
You did a decent thing that hardened to a lie.
I took your name because going to the ovens
you had no more need of it than clothes.
I was a young goblin—you said an angel—
I never thought I'd be watching you
with as much love as you had for me,
and once I knew it was my lot, how
could I have known it would be so hard?
I'm as brave a watcher as you're a fool—
you can't always win at craps or fake a life.
If you're lame you limp, if mutilated
you can only pretend. You suffered cruelty:

people who couldn't be bothered called it the breaks—
so let's call those breaks beyond repair.
You're beyond repair, what's left of you.
That has been your condition for a long time.
You tried to steal home on one leg
and the ghouls in the stands encouraged you.
You exiled your witness and called it growing up.
Sitting in a pool of blood, you couldn't prove the crimes.
What am I going to do with you
now I've seen your song is sung?

II

You lost your heart for the slog.
Did you foresee it unfold?
You chose to die back there
in a privet chapel where we prayed
toward the U-boats off Great South Bay.
I think that when I left you
to weed my Chinese cabbage I knew
you'd be gone when I came back.
I kept on talking as if you were there,
I knew you'd quit and taken my name,
and because there was no more you
it didn't matter what anyone called me.
The wrongness of your decision darkens me:
you should have lived this life,
you were the strong invisible one,
you would have known what to do.
You left me to a world that revolted you.
How could I prosper in it?
No one would have expected my wound to heal
—chin up, soldier on, and all that blah—
but who expected you to fall down?
I would have carried you all this way.
Instead I have your desertion to bear.
You understood the wounds were grave,
I knew just enough to be a revenant.

If I had to guess at your despair
after these sixty years I'd say
it was because you couldn't make me weep.
I know you tried, I know you left a sob
in my chest that never dissolved in the tumult
of ordinary life. A sob to remember you by,
a sob and my failure to weep.
Whoever corrupts a child deafens him to angels
and sets him down among demons.

III

Stars electric swarm
a privet chapel where
a boy prays for wings to leave
leaden bloodiness here.

If all those guardians could ignore
bloody sheets and clothes,
gasp and wheeze and disappearance
of a smile replaced by a sob
that in a child is euphemism
for the implosion of a star,
then to grow up is to clean up
evidence of the cruelest crimes.

Religion forbidden here,
miracles and savaged children
only are allowed. Wonder,
stigmata and wings
accepted conditions. Words
suspect but permitted
in emergencies such as these.

Wiping his tears on Aisling's underwear

I wouldn't want to be you.
After you I didn't want to be me.

There was no light behind you, no getting by you,
nothing, nobody, nowhere to go to.

Even today after all this
there is nothing but you,
a giantess then, now a basin of the sea.
I'm Odysseus and Sindbad plying your briny whims,
I'm Robert Ballard laying out a grid,
hoisting artifacts from the anaerobic muck of your navel,
Aeneas betraying Dido.

With inappropriate touch you forfeited
commerce with an angel, with profane scent,
operatic strut, you killed the child
in your safekeeping, and a ruined creature
wiped his tears with your underwear.

We had to be each other's hauntings,
brokenness and disconnection, thanks
to your intrusions, and you weren't even drunk,
although my own drunkenness was born
in your bedroom, now a Pentecostal pile of brick.

To these late iterations of you I say,
don't play with my hair unless you like me,
don't count on my being used to crumbs,
don't assume I came here with amnesia,
don't even try to pass as a trifler—
I feel the malevolence in your fingertips.

I may look like a child, in spite of my white hair,
but I'm that element immune to your elixirs,
and all you've done to me is future rot
where you expected pleasure. I'm busy
scattering your privacies on the next-door lawn.

Aisling's robe

If you punish me for a sin
you say I know but won't admit
you count on the severe weather
of my mind to cover your tracks.

If your robe falls open and I
forget you are about to strike
you count on me to learn too late
that nothing is an accident.

Your beauty baffled me;
I thought I had to do something
to keep it on an even keel,
keep it from being my problem.

I don't know why you beat me. Your scents
even now fill dripping alleys
with irresistible foreboding.
I see the dim light where you wait,

the one room where I shouldn't be.
The others are filled with strangers,
and you, the strangest of them all,
are sadly most familiar to me.

This is not about forgiveness,
not about anything so final;
it is about stopping your hand
mid-air and looking at me.

Where he grew old

I hope this night will pass before I do,
meanwhile two white carnations and a lily
stand watch with me, and by the way,
where will the night go, especially
if as some physicists now say
there is no spacetime? The TV is off
not just so I can write this or hear geese honk outside,
but because I'm trying to recollect
certain body odors and chilling acts
that etched upon my face the certainty
no good comes of letting anyone in
to an inner space I myself distrust.
I don't know if it was a crib misgiving
or something a long time arriving
from another galaxy, but it lit
Aisling's bedroom when I was a boy
and then and there I grew old,
incapable of a thousand pleasures
give or take a few mistakes,
and all those conversations I've had
even when I wasn't drunk come down
to sorting out what happened then
when Aisling's robe fell open purposefully
and my innocence poured out.

The train is wailing on its way to Albany,
I don't think I'll ever see Montreal.
The lily thanks me for my body heat,
the carnations were cut like me and drink
still waters, and the pictures on the wall

will not hang straight, crooked as they are,
like my caretakers and Aisling's face—
No one is symmetrical but some of us
in our asymmetry are beautiful,
and I wonder if anyone ever thought me so.
I've worshipped beauty as a museum visitor
and but for Aisling I might have worshipped it
intimately, at night, or somewhere
less disposed to authority, unguarded
and actually happy I was there.

Your hurricane holes

I want to take refuge in your hurricane holes,
sail upheavals of your navel, rappel
your nether secrecies, study the cockatoos
of your jungles, stare into your volcanoes,
and if after such excitements there is rest
for Lilliputians like me, let it be
in the torrents of your sorrows running
to the abyss in which our suppositions
float like continental corpses—worlds
in which the dying mourn in half light
ancient lovers and vows that rise
like shattered masts in watery crypts,
want, I want, want to sleep not this insomnia
of the lost child grown old in an hour,
bleeding of rape and indifference,
shocked to obsequy and despair.
How do such children wake, how
are they not too awake, awake
to every snapping branch, footfall,
creak and turn of key?

Remorseless as an autistic child

Each recognition becomes a pixel,
the portrait emerges unbearable—
enhance, retouch, crop, lighten,
export to some blocked synapse
where you live back to the wall
pretending to be an insider
but seeing as the camera sees,
remorseless as an autistic child.

I could go on about this
acuity of the Leica lens, but
life is photo-shopped except
for those who never give the image over
so as not to betray the child
who chose to believe what he saw
not what beguilers said he saw
or how adults interpreted it.

The child admits enough light to probe
worlds in the cracks of smooth facades.
We teach to shut the little camera down.

Note to Aisling

You're not in people's way,
you just come across that way,
as if you're on a collision course
when you've signaled safe passage.

I've puzzled this out about you
and I think it has to do
with the impulse to ruin a child
who seems too free and wild.

Pip's Islips

Were it not for shape memory in my cock
there'd be no Queensboro to erect
to the Astorias of my desires, the grudgelands
between the towers and the sea would crawl
with honking incidents and sting
the sore carcass of my brain rifling
cardboard suitcases in forsaken attics
in the sunken Islips of a childhood
ruined by the itchy fingers of the dead.

Pip's warning

Gutters in all that I write.
I can't find my way out of it,
can't spell or form the vowels
that would whoosh through
the keyhole of it, splashing
memories on a floor waiting
for the footprints of archaeologists;
life is archaeology full
of Sutton Hoos and Stonehenges,
and all our getting rich is
neglect and cowardice. I swear
what I never will write
is all I try to write, but who
will pin a medal on me for that
or wire a check to my account?
My name is the number of that account.
All you who fingered me,
diddled me, messed me over,
pronounce me at your peril.

Pip's wickedness

I

I'm not like that,
yoking a woman with fake affection
in the public street,
terrified of loss
as if vulgar possession
is anything but illusion.
I'm too wicked for that,
even as a little boy,
the acrid pretense
of well-wishers
spoiled me for society.
This one thing the ruined boy knew,
this unholy thing:
to covet is to kill,
and so we must let be,
adoring the scented with sorrow.

How did the ruined boy know?
By his resolve, I think, to be unlike
invaders wearing familial faces
or victims of the Holocaust
in which our children are Jews
or gypsies experimented on.
He wouldn't be an experiment,
knowing as he knew when to leave.
But there are only so many somewheres to go,
and so he happens to walk behind
them as she turns and he notices
she's not as possessed as her possessor thinks.

II

I see with a wicked eye,
wicked in its love
of lifting up the skirts
of settled matters
and redefining them in ways
that incite history to riot.

Hello, little do you know
I've just written a poem about you
in an effort to free you of your thingyness,
or do you know,
know in some way that scatters words like egrets
standing on a water–chestnut isle
as insubstantial as belief?

Halfling's rest

And then nothing ever happened
or, being nothing, could have been,
but as I waited for it to happen
I found peace in becoming part of it,
becoming it as it was becoming to me,
and all my restlessness stood
in front of me as someone else's stress,
someone rising from the bottom
of a glacial tarn, not exactly a former self
but a person no one wanted me to be,
a drowned person consenting to be me.
not exactly did I weight him down
and row away, not exactly was I myself,
and now I celebrate this inexactly because
it is the trysting glade of ghosts.

When our parents were bothering us

Can't find the book or the look
lost in a crowd of impressions
perched on the ledges of my head.
I will be all right, it will end well
if I can find it, but I'm afraid
the house will burn down first
or the cleaning lady took it
and is infected with my entities
posing as my identities
in which case I should feel better
or at least not like a murder of crows
tasked to build a glittery nest
for the pleasure of Ahriman.
It's a simple predicament,
obsessive-compulsive disorder,
afflicting people who can't trust
anything to hold its shape
or resemble what it's supposed to be.
So, about the book, you know what,
I wish it luck in its viper pit
of success and fame, luck feeling naked
in the company of crowds and crows.
I walk backwards fast. And that look,
I read too much into it, it read
too much into me, and we
made time to grow up and be
something like the elementals we saw
dancing around ice cream wagons
when our parents were bothering us.

In me

In me in me inme

When he stuck it in me, when Aisling tutored him,
I studied the purplish cloth of the telephone cord
when it happened, when I was split apart,
when I was taken apart, aware, unaware, taken
somewhere I did and did not want to go, when
something was taken from me I did not give
and yet would have given if I knew how.
I've read all about it in the books. Nothing fits.
It's not what I felt staring at that purplish cord,
not what I feel a lifetime later. Nothing fits.
I said then what I had to say, a gasp
was my definitive utterance. This, this
gardener's hygiene, picking spent flowers,
a gardener's farewell, is all I make of it, all I know.
I know this about all other boys and men,
they're not Pip. I'm sure of other Aislings,
but I've avoided them, having been so well forewarned,
and yet she did, did she not, put Pip in me,
an act for which I'm not entirely ungrateful.
Perhaps some things are meant to happen only once.
Well, that's not exactly the way it was. There was,
I'm sure of it, a sense we lost as much as we gained
and would live as cripples improvising. I notice
they use the term work-around now. I worked around
what happened to me, to us, to us three, three,
because I doubt Aisling got off free. But why
didn't we look each other up, since looking back
would characterize our lives? Maybe each of us
architects built a memory palace of dismay
we didn't want to profane as tourists. Maybe.

In me in me in me in me, painfully, shudderingly,
help me, please, don't stop, rescue me
from I'm not sure what, this strange softness,
this terrifying hardness, help! And then what?
The bleeding, aching cold, the shivering
in Aisling's arms, two of us, three of us,
me and Pip growing up, drunk
on her scent, our own, frightened, spent.

You, forever in me, and that purplish cloth
through which no message pulsed except
perhaps our pleas for somewhere else,
for this, for that, for what was happening,
pleas of what? Innocence, guilt? We would be gone,
the three of us, the two of us, all of us,
did we think of that or did we think
we would never be gone? Never gone,
that was true, that is true. We are all over us,
salve and irritant, balm and scent, ghostly
hands still fondling us, fondling each other
to our graves. Aisling, Pip, Sally.
I did not sally forth, I remain a sally port
between what we were and could never be,
between a time I didn't think so innocent
what with all my itches, soiled panties,
sly glances, humors, whims, wants, wonts,
and the rest of this life … is it shame,
my ingenious making use
of what happened in that hot room
to grow flowers, tell lies, and on occasion
tell a truth nobody can forgive me for?
After Aisling put Pip in me I was always
that girl, that woman who's going to say
something you've been dreading, that woman
who's going to hang ink in the air,
but it didn't make a paranoid of me, no,
it made of me a priestess, bent, ruthless,
but inclined to do good, to grow flowers,

take care of the wounded, and even
have a few love affairs. Do I blame Aisling?
For what? Being crazy, like her parents,
austere paragons of righteousness
who could not have known as little
as we gave them credit for, or as much
as they took credit for.

That thing

Away, get it away,
get that thing away from me.
I must have it as much as it must have me,
get it away, and that's how my life will be—
stuck, clogged, hurting there.

The words don't come, they're not there,
they're lost in a tunnel,
not that it was exquisite,
that moment left back there,
but that it didn't leave voluntarily—
we were torn away, thrown back
into a childhood blackened
by what happened, yes,
that's how to describe
that sexual ballet choreographed
by that witch-priestess,
that experiment in which innocence
was sucked out of us.

No words come, just the music,
terrifying, dragging us
back there into that tunnel
where we can't breathe,
here where a sob devours us.

Be bold to say

Child of unrest, child most blest,
come, black-light invisible ink,
come, be adored and crucified,
reborn in every child, die
and be reborn until each pupil
bears your face and we can bear
such light as now we glimpse
in vanishing glances and corners
engulfed by advancing night.

I hear you faintly through almond scent
inducing what I hope is sleep.
Blood is hard to clean up,
life is Luminol, hydrogen peroxide helps,
religion salves, and death
is not as restful as we think.

What can I getcha ya, hon?
Getcha ain't gotcha, Lord.
Do this in remembrance of me.
Doowuh for whom, who he?
This is my body, hon, take,
eat this in remembrance,
but what if that remembrance …
what if drunk on that remembrance
I stagger to the altar unable
to keep the feast, any feast?
What if instead of taking heart
I squeak in my shoes and fart?

What can you get me, hon?
Hold my hand as I die on this tiled floor
that hosted fire engines once.
This is my body, hon, take, eat,
do this for the remembrance
of a ten-year-old on her bike,
a sea-grass field, an endless day
before the getchas and gotchas got you.

And as for my blood, if
it should make you eternal,
vampire or angel, remember me
when the neon sputtered out
and nothing would stay lit,
and the train wailed in the night.
Remember me as you illicitly
pressed me to your muff,
you being whom I die not to speak.
Remember me. Do this, be bold to say
we can't bear each other's night
or make ourselves at home
in each other's pupils or stay
with each other a little while
in this grotesque Gethsemane waiting
for recognitions to arrive.

I know my breath smells like almonds
promising what I hope is sleep,
I'll leave you a big tip—bet on remembering
where you left your bike in the fen,
by what inlet, and then remember
I'm still there waiting for you
before all this happened, this
kerfuffle covering up the crime.

Scarlet fever

I don't like to be touched
said it said it said it
& I'm not even beautiful
say it say it say it
but I pretended that I do
pretended pretended pretended
til 4 in the mourning
of the last days of my life
however many they will be
til this reckoning
behind my navel where
bile is stored & burbles
from what was a freshet
when I didn't need glasses
& hadn't yet doused scarlet fever
in winters of denial.

What if I had been a mannequin?

What if I have been a mannequin?
What then will I have briefly seen,
a predator who lost his taste for meat?
What digestion did I wear?
Was it fashionable?
Who touched me inappropriately
knowing I would be unmoved?
I was expected to be moved,
but on occasion passersby
noticed being noticed
and might have even seen me smile
or register a tic.
That's the way it is with us children left for dead.
You'd better dress us up who knew us naked well
and when they raise the rent and you move on
you'd better not leave us in the dumpster
for some poor artist to find
and paint our testament.

Sally remembers Ludilon

I like its reflection in the water more than the boat;
that's how I've always spent my gaze,
thinking the image is too bright,
seeing it as if waiting for its eclipse,
preferring its reflection to itself
not only to save my eyes but to savor
its emanations and their interplay
with surfaces that otherwise repel me.

Your story is written on the water
as if it depends on being erased,
and there's its worth and writ,
and the duty of reflective things.
I learned this as a child when I saw
girls assuring themselves in windows
that they exist beyond the expectations
of others. I fell in love with them,
or, more properly I should say
with their understanding
nothing they were told is true.

Playing with herself

A wild pinky flees the work at hand
striking an erotic chord
that shatters the demeanor
of the human beast.

It's the symbol of our predicament
that we don't wish to be doing
what we do so well and seek
alternatives pointlessly
as if our lives depend on it.

Here we pray for the voyeur
to rescue us from our privacy,
to deliver us from inwardness,
or for the mirror to rebel
against such hard usage.

Years ago in Babylon

No one should have to walk from the restroom past the bar.
Too much face to put on, demeanor not our own
reminding us of all we've had to recover from,
all the scrutinies we did not get by, and when we arrive
at the table how to resume the life we left sitting there,
the ice water we meant to spill into someone's lap,
pretending to be sorry, not meaning to come back?

No one should have to contend with bartenders,
look-at-me's hanging on, pee on the toilet seat, husbands,
or the terrible antisepsis of going along
when you want to burn the place to the ground
and piss on embers from a great height to cook a witchy fume.

No one should have to observe hundred-proof protocols
as if there were a norm or be hindered by a name
as if we're our luggage. No one. Not you. Not her,
the one still making nice and explaining you.

Go back through the kitchen into the alley and let
your companions wipe up the uncompanionable mess.
Walk—you've had a little too much recognition to drive—
along the river, back to the rooms where eidolons play
as you left them because you thought you had to be
somewhere else, someone else, and now you've come to
the river's teeming orgasms, come to a girl who looking
in a plate glass window years ago in Babylon, and seeing
no one, never mentions it, not even to herself.

Sally's perfumery

I have that anxious genome.
Aromas of marble and people,
their scents and senses afflicting,
dizzy me, and on a good day
that means staggering instead
of a dignified stride, but then
there is transfiguration, holiness
in being one with whatever
that one is, and not even death
overshadows such a moment.
The world is my perfumery.
Nothing sobers that genome.
It is fatal, sunlight to a vampire,
worse than any grand compulsion,
inheritance preceding the imposters
who claimed to be my parents.
The world is my perfumery
and they knew it even before
I stood up in the crib, knew
I would not be a decorative curse.

Kerosene of sorrows

Nothing appeals to us as much as lies,
not even gods and goddesses, because
they don't need us as much.
They can shape other creatures,
bowl other balls, move
other pieces on the cosmic square,
so we masturbate
with our lies, our plastic devices
eaten by the kerosene
of sorrows, and it shortens
our lives, this love of lies,
shortens us when we could tower,
because we wouldn't swim the pores,
wander the forests of their bodies,
and so we're stuck between their toes.

Under Sally's bed

I dropped a sweater on the floor,
a piece of it slunk away.
I don't believe this any more than you
and yet I testify that room forebodes
brushes with the scents of abandoners.

A creature departed me
and now consorts with long-eyed ones
who, shaking off my judgment,
invite me to cavort
as if we'd never met before.

Death sends ornate invitations
current occupants intercept,
perhaps a feline messenger,
and death is not amused that I
prefer to sleep under the bed.

Sally's chapel

It has never bothered me that doorknobs come off
in my hand. I can imagine my way through
keyholes or humor the impenetrable. Neither
doors nor boxes beguile me, nor have my
animosities ever been toxic enough
to poison anybody or be an anti-venom.
I have for the most part been exhaust
slinking under doors, through cracked windows
and the seams and stitches of disguises. I have
narrowed my pupils too little, let in too much
and had to deal with alchemies that madness
goes sane to spite. It has all been like playing
hooky from Sunday school, praying in my
privet chapel for adults to die
and being unconcerned about consequences
as if lightning would strike at noon and I
would be sent to bed without supper,
a dead girl animated by something acrid
and metallic, an attractant to others of my kind.

Sally speaks of harm

Is it in my behalf you stick
something in someone else
or stick yourself in me?
Exactly where, exactly what
& with what degree of intimacy,
since this smells of sexuality,
or is this foofaraw and rime?
Wind carries it like pollen
when someone has it in for me.
I sneeze or rub my side
or take a sudden chill, a sense
someone is standing behind me
or staring at me across the room,
but still I don't know what it is,
I can't arrange my body
to receive the blow or as in aikido
use an assailant's thrust
to handle him, and I'm balked
by not wanting to hurt anyone
or knowing what I should have
taken in or taken out or held harmless
by those who would harm me
for the harm they see in me.

Sally's stammer

All I wanted was to be held,
the rest I cooked up for effect,
held, not invaded, not titillated,
but the shame of so modest a plea
blew fuses and short-circuited me.
A man's supposed to be ambitious,
to conquer, acquire wealth, be felt;
I worried about being felt up.
I had good reason but I stuttered
in my head and words came out
as if a liar had crumbled them,
so I had to hug him, hold his head,
although he was not my child.
That's how it is with us devil-worshippers,
us split babies unable to grow up,
stuck in someone's reverie,
glowing in that light. Hold me,
take your chances, I may rub out
your ineradicable sob and set
you free to light up galaxies.

Sally's thighs

Fiddle kept the tableware in place
through squall and foundering,
but the charts were ruined, the bilges awash,
and half a pint of Kinsey
bobbed against the pumps.
Sea oats leaned leeward, the sun played
on Sally's thighs,
and the two of us imagined havens
where *Ludilon* might take us
away from desires not quite as dangerous
as our own.
Not sailors or lovers yet,
we knew nothing beyond Fire Island
would be better than this if only
we knew what to do with it, and when we kissed,
never having thought of whiskey,
we saw the abyss in each other's eyes
and knew we'd always be able to say
one day lying in the tall grass,
crab nets at our feet, Gaia blinked,
but we didn't, and after that day
life was commentary.
We'd come here for a moment
that turned our world into hiraeth,
and only the crass would say
we fumbled it.

Sally remembers Pip

He never looks as if he wants to do something else
or looks for someone else over your shoulder.
His demeanor's a clock tower's, its unheard rollback
before striking is his repose. For him it's always time,
always your moment and his. Your encounter
is a 20-mile wave cresting at the foot of a Ferris wheel.
You are cast up like spume to his propitious gaze
and both of you are refreshed. You are his cross—
he was born to be crucified and multiplied
by your witness. Remember when you were a child
feeling that something had to happen, someone?
Remember feeling later it would be sexual?
This is your proof. Have you forgotten it already?
Did it happen while you were preoccupied
with marking papers, buying a car, having sex?
It doesn't matter. It will come back to you
in a dream, a time as unexpected as when it came,
because you are the X of the moment, the cross
and that is why nothing ever rings quite true
and no one seems right to you. You were waiting
and although you think you overlooked him that day
you did in fact prove the necessity of the zero
to higher math—you were born a fey saltire.

Aisling's inlet

A boy is watching us

Thoughts infecting me acted on their own,
I celebrated the disease. He was seven
when my robe fell open. No one else
will ever own him. This is all I know at root.
He was mine, he smelled me, and I spanked him
for some made-up offense. His real offense
was seeing me without intent, with eyes
that didn't belong in anyone's head and were bound
to get him in trouble in my lap and everywhere
corruptors sweat in the presence of children
who've accidentally landed here.
I picked him out because I could, being resident god,
and the singular honor bewitched him,
as it should, so he came to chapel often
to worship face down at my altar.
I gave him sacred privileges but couldn't keep
him to myself. Others craved and ruined him.
I've never told a lover a boy is watching us,
touching in me what no one else can find.
I bet my taste will haunt his ashes. Is he gone?
I would know, it would be a numbness.
We were awake. Can the moral say as much?
The school is now a fundamentalist church—
do you think their solvents rid them of our scent?
I'd repent if I hadn't been his luck. I hope
he knows some of us are visitors, not subject
to the ways you bore yourselves to death,
subject to what we get away with and only
if it illumines something in the night.

Aisling's look and thicket

There's always the hook in the closet
under the stairs waiting for you
to hang your life on it and go on
acting as if you're having one:
the one whom you let loom too large,
who didn't succumb to your charms,

who walked off wiping your blood away,
that one has become the hook, and you
tread up and down on what was your life
knowing you've hung it in the dark to mold.
Everyone reminds us of someone else,
everything is redolent of something else,

each of us uses a different language.
The familiar is what's agreed upon
in order not to be lost in each other's thickets,
and only instant touch or glance imparts
your entire code to another on a dare
no one has seen or sensed but you.

Aisling to Pip

I have tried bravely to like you
(your decency's not well hidden);
it shames me to fail and yet
the pleasure of it itches
the parts I've hidden best.

How can I hurt you with this news,
you with your platinum antennae,
and why did you hope against hope,
knowing I chose you to dislike?
I blame you for this mean game,

for wanting to hang around
watching my contortions
as I scratched what you inflamed.
Yes you, you're not an innocent,
you're a sexual predator.

Aisling's inlet

Strychnine childhood on the banks
of Wynant's Inlet plucking mussels
baiting crabs with pork rinds

sugarcoated childhood
gathering algae to fertilize
sandy fields of denial

strychnine seeds & sugar laced
with cyanide & arsenic
smiley facing doping us
with beatitudes that crumbled
in our honed sight

tricking crabs and getting
raped & otherwise initiated
into the mysteries of adult behavior

raped comforted reassured
it was for our own good our
schooling in the ways
of suffocation supplication
to improve our lungs.

Do you know
what strychnine death is like
or how many of us are resurrected?
Do you know, have you touched
our ineradicable sobs
our charred short-circuitries?

I confuse the scent of Great South Bay
with Aisling's inlet not the one

out there but in this suffocation room
the scent of her occurrences the ones
she orchestrated in this musty room
stupefied with her perfume.

I confuse what happened
with what I wish had happened
with interrupted dreams
sleepwalk fevers & the lie.

I imagined it as if
I knew what it was laced
with suffering the little children
to come unto her between her knees
but not to come to
under any circumstance not
to wake up and understand—
what could we understand?

I confuse what's happening with
the profanities Sally and I performed
discharged
under Aisling's tutelage tasks tastes fragrances
flagrances drumming in our hearts
gasps sobs and Aisling's giant insistencies.

And afterwards afterwords
what did we know except
no one else was that boy that girl
or ever could be and we were spoiled
for anyone else
spoiled
even for ourselves
and what was Aisling then but a lie
a towering lie whose Cycladian head we couldn't see
whose eyes were now taboo to us
who'd seen so much and were to go on our way
as if nothing happened except
that now we knew not even tides could be trusted

and something is always about to happen
something that will be denied
and we will never be able to explain
how something was pulled out of us
instructively extracted
that no one nothing could replace.

Strychnine childhood and overdose
accidental as being pincered from a womb
strychnine childhood in that room
which while not fatal might as well have been
and then a life of eating almonds for their arsenic
staring into everyone for an end
& not finding enough cyanide
in the stone of the peach.

Hymn to Aisling

Grinding the wrong powder,
dropping it in the wrong vial
year after year and then
Venus slips the horns of the crescent,
the nightscape falls back
illuminating one whose robe
opens to reveal that galaxy,
the one from which you came,
and now no further entries need
be entered in the log,
no further ciphers scribbled
in the margins—all is clear.
Look up and let the stars
re-constellate your mind,
restore it to its lost position
in the firmament you always
heard above the din—
that hum celestial, forbearing
and amazingly bereft of you.

The suffocating room

A mother wouldn't do this,
not to any woman's child,
unless her demons swallowed his
and she needed to expose her belly
still digesting them—wouldn't,
shouldn't, it doesn't matter
until an explosion more brilliant
than our mother star devours them
and they become pinpricks of light
playing on the skin of innocents
they've yet to meet. Too late,
too late for them for talk
of sin, redemption, forgiveness,
the usual blather. All that's left
is a sere plain not yet refined
to desert—and an ineradicable sob.

In envy of youth

In the silence of the wizened,
gardens strewn with body parts,
there's more truth than is written.
Time is to and fro, back and forth,
not clink, clunk and tick, not tyranny
but what is coming to be and has been
ennobling what we encounter.
Study them, ruins in which repose
all that was loved and uttered
and is wise enough now not to speak—
eternal putti holding up the frame
in which we exhibit youth burning
on scaffolds built of envy.
So much evil is done in envy of youth
we'd rather blow up the planet than cop to it.
No wonder we despise silence,
our native tongue, preferring
to speak the language of mercenaries
in the service of usurper kings
selling us useless things in the name
of gods we know are phonies.

We wear antlers at night

To live forty or fifty years as a beauty
differs from living them beautifully;
to have to look for meaning elsewhere
is heroic beyond all means to define.
There is no failing or succeeding at this
elemental task; it's too ennobling
for all that palaver, for politics. Youth
is a fitting out for that one thing, an elixir
that turns crud to emeralds in time
no calendar can measure, time spent,
we're deluded into thinking, we can describe
when no logbook, no novel, no painting
can reveal a second of it, so sacred
are its rites and obligations, so secret
we despair of knowing one another, making
whole religions to prove we do, because
in the dark of the night we know we wear
antlers and creaturely things so frightening
they can only be seen in the etheric light
of the wilderness where our companion lives.

Cajoling golems out

Children see but cannot say
who is making love with ghosts
in ruined upstairs windows.
Children see the writing on the wall,
the tortures thoughts endure
as they're beaten into words.
Children feel the summoning
of elementals in the woods.
Children see our true intent
before we correct our faces.
Children see but cannot say
all we teach them to deny,
and in their anguish they become
artists, poets and murderers.
Did we not murder them
and cajole their golems out
to lie about the crime?

Aisling's throes

Bezel earth with awe,
wear it around your neck
on a necklace of dreams.

As you voyage Aisling's throes,
sail your consonants hauling
amphorae of vowels,

hoist pennants of diacriticals
to signal harbormasters
of your goings and comings,

plot glacial melt
and lava to her groins,
and in those vortices exult

in noctilucent clouds
that needed cold and height
to reveal phantoms.

I must brush them away
to draw beasts star to star
on blackboards swarming

with equations half-remembered—
they distract me, I forget
my feet to lose my mind

beneath your neckline
where lilac sleeps, but honeysuckle
impairs judgment

patriotically. I persist,
and after a while a dragon,
eyes a mercy of black holes,

civilizations in its teeth,
kneels like a camel
for someone like me to mount

and my voyage to your navel
on twenty-mile rollers of sweat,
seasick and giddy

with the labor of words,
is done, and I disembark,
dizzy in enemy morning.

Aisling Wynant's panties down

Call them back
in fussy disarray:
Eleanor R & Earle J,
maple fire & apple whiff,
clamshell and coal ash
driveway, their daughter
Aisling's widowed whim,
her sloe-eyed muskiness
& a boy's fright
in boarding school
at being unable to do
what was required of him
illegally & ruinously.

Call them back
to what purpose now
from the organ loft
where pigeons roost,
rag dolls rot,
back from recognition
all occasions are not
to rise to and some
fragrances are so illicit
as to sear soul from eyes?

Lift the hem of institutions
to find Aisling Wynant's
panties down
and all that ceremony
nothing but her quim.

Bail to crucifix

I've lived more years than there are rosary beads,
what has the supermoon to do with this?
As much as my parents had with me.
I'm the 60th and uncomplaining bead.
Lament is not complaint.
But I have not always been happy to be fingered
by those praying for someone else
or to be bail to crucifix.
I've been wrapped around someone's hand,
arraigned on someone's lap,
and expected to be the magic by which clouds
are levered up and histories expunged.
Will the supermoon dissolve
my supple arrangements, absolve
my many failures to deliver on my promises?
Wouldn't it be nice to hear someone say
I swear I left the damned thing here,
nicer still if here need not imply there?
Moonlight is counting me backwards
to the clasp. When it gets there,
among the succulents on the table,
will there be an observance of my last gasp?

A room that devours light

Mouth agape, arm outstretched
in a room that devours light.
Can you tell us what happened?
You sound just like the ones
I'm trying to tell you about.
But you haven't said a thing
until now. It's not the room,
it's you, absorbing light,
scrubbing walls with solvent lies.
I may have had a stroke
or by a stroke of luck I sense
the inhumanity in your skin.
You won't trifle with me again.
I will be done, not you.
Become a petal or a snowflake
in the maelstrom of memories
explorers must trek through.
I'll freeze on their eyelashes,
drop off their noses in such
a high degree of awareness
they'll note something eerie
in their journals, like heat
rising from a crevasse.

If I smell of it

You wouldn't have been caught dead
walking around this town at night.

I've been caught dead in more interesting places
and seen others of my ilk marrying
all sorts of you. When you say you
you're out of your league, fashing us
with synthetic personhoods.
I'm my own alchemical lab,
stirring the nobilities of the dead
with body fluids of pronouns like you.

Wouldn't have been caught dead?
With what word do you distance yourself
from wraiths? I apologize,
you were just making conversation,
and here I had to traffick
in the nature of being caught,
the idle accusative, the scent of ilk
and such esoteric things as to prompt
you to avoid me in the street
as I shop in the cemeteries of things,
damned pilings up of accoutrements.
Damn me, damn me all to hell.
Use Lysol on me if I smell of it.

I wasn't being as innocent as you thought,
I was trying to itch you into song,
and if I gag on what you've said
it's because I caught you dead when you thought
you had me fooled, dead in the crib

rotting slowly in my mind
like a rat in the wall. And now you apologize
as if death hadn't taught you much.
Who is it who is fooled?

The most troubling angel

The most troubling angel

I can't see you were you not unseen.

Even now I see only parts of you,
    each glance intrusion, theft.

My respect for you rests on this—
    if I saw everything
        the odor of exploded ego
            would take my place.

That's why God is a vowel
    not a cocky consonant
        prodding a howl somewhere.

The most troubling angel is light,
    lifting the hem of things,
        troubling intervals and interstices.

Let's not hold still to be seen.

Nothing owns its own shape
    or owns up to what it's not.

No one.

And we must bathe
    in that awe and refresh
        our childish determination,
            not learn innocence away, not
                for parents' convenience or
                    to accommodate swindlers.

It's a curse whatever else it is to be seen.

Blessed be that all
    that is most of all unseen.

Spell of evil spent

A little boy was violated there
in what is now a janitor's closet
of high-rise anonymity
and we should have no doubt
that crime can't be washed out
or carted away, but in the street
we assign its chill to someone
staring at us from behind
or a meeting we've missed
and in that way we excuse
the stench of possession.
We huff our shoulders up
and pretend to be offended
by something innocent to dispel
the scent of wickedness,
the spell of evil spent.

Of which we're redolent

We're all facsimiles of ourselves,
the best excuses we can make
for not being quite, yet making do
thanks to photographs, paintings
and descriptions that seem
like someone we once knew,
someone sent away, evacuated
so we that we might face this alone,
this whatever it is that haunts us
here in the aftermath of an encounter
of which we're redolent.

Stumbling on their lairs

Memories come like golems in the dark
to jolt your ancient crib. Scents arise
like vipers to strike when you stumble
on their lairs, and you're held in the eye
of the moment, shuddering as if
you'd never learned to walk or utter
a pathetic squawk and then thunder
shakes the house and lightning shows
wan creatures writhing to get in—
you will always panic that they will
and that will stand in for your life,
that panic impersonating someone
bearing your name—which becomes
more foreign by the day until
your heart booms and swats your breath away.

What is erased

We are each other's impossibilities
slithering over to our toes, S-shaped,
quick, unwilling to be grasped,
poignant beyond belief because
we know we are too slow,
not as gainly as other beasts,
slippery in our pride.
Whatever scuttles, slithers
and slides across the floor
bereaves us and suggests
how uncivilized we are.
We are what is erased
from chalkboards before
we have worked it out,
and our nostalgia is so great
it impugns our every word
and makes of periods sorrows.

Why should I tap my fingers?

Rape never clears the cache.
Installing: Eighteen minutes remaining:
why should I tap my fingers considering
how long it's taken to instill
awareness of the enemy within,
the child refusing to believe
the frozen smiles that kept breaking off
and clattering on the floor, the reassurances
of love in its buzzing absence?
Eighteen minutes remaining?
It's not that my sight never clarified
or that my ears shut out
words that twisted lips leaving them,
no, it's that pretense seemed
as elemental as breath. I was convinced
updating my operating system meant
some fatal virus would get in, convinced
in spite of a mysterious grin signaling.
I knew what's fatal—parenthood, promises,
all we beat out of children to extort from them
evidence they believe us. I was put in harm's way,
that's what rape made of me, a contemplative
who finally came to see God's in me,
I am absolution and as much transcendence
as this motherboard can bear without short-circuiting.

Newcomer's progress

Each switchback is steeper than the last.
Roots impede the newcomer's progress,
and the promise of belonging sets
behind farther hills, leaving him to commune
with star beasts descending for purposes
he's too breathless to fathom.
Breathe with Gaia on her breast,
she doesn't ask if you deserve the rest.

Longboats questing

A light too hot to touch
turns our thoughts to cinders.
Lies protect us from the flames,
cool our ardors and ought
with a little machination
make civil servants of us.
Light maddens us for truth,
truth, that wilding spree,
axe-swinging berserker,
snatcher of maiden reveries,
dragging them by the hair
to the longboats questing.
We prefer shadows, but not
their shades, creatures
preparing us to eat, not
light too hot to hope
for something more than lies,
something if not paradise
akin to walking upright,
talking straight, seeing
life ought to be epiphany.

They're not you

The problem is they're not you
and that second we were one never came
and therefore keeps on coming,
and their most distinguishable mark
is that they're not you
and we two notes in a bottle bob
in oceans of roiling years
thrown time and again by breakers
on rocks that always fall away
rescued from curious hands,
never delivered in any sense of the word.

Cache

It wasn't under the floor
or sewn into a stuffed bunny,
it didn't catch a glance of light;
it came to me a high note
from a musty choir, white
as moonlight on an icy pond.
If a countertenor had sung it
I'd gasp. Eight altar candles
would gutter. But it touched
my hand and whispered,
Do you know my name? Yes,
I said, your name is Grace
and you have blown out
the yearning in my face
for someone to distract me
from becoming numen
whose breaths measure
wanting less and knowing
that is being's treasure.

Build a cello

Build a cello in which to live,
an instrument whose harmonics
make you a hymn to guardians,
forty thousand of them yearning
for your ear after millennia
of ancestral meddling—pillagers

messing with you in bed,
rearranging the furnishings
of your head to mislead you
in your mistakes. And then,
praying with sharpened stone,
a shaman to yourself, you cut

the milky way connecting you
to your delusions and bow
the strings of your new dwelling
across the bridges of the mind
as if you were born deserving it
and the world had sung alleluia.

Ludilon
A short novel

Well, that's that then, Sally, take care.

Well, that's that then, Sally, take care? You came here from God-knows-where after all this time to sputter that?

I guess so, yeah.

She'd run out into the faint rain, shouting, Rain, rain, go away, come another day. She knew it would stop him in his tracks, someone calling him Rain, a nickname very few people ever heard or used. His name was Philip Didschus. Most people called him Pip. She called him Rain because he loved to stand in the rain, any kind of rain. He'd climb up on the slick slate roofs of Galilee, the barn, the icehouse or the schoolhouse, and sit like a gargoyle in the rain, even when it turned to hail. So she called him Rain, and once, just once, he'd smiled.

Now it stops him. He stands facing the traffic, hesitating to face her. Then he turns. A streetlight illuminates his raptor's face. He's much taller than she remembers, but she's almost as tall. There's that familiar stillness in his body—that look of being about to take wing. She'd picked him out of her audience as if Galilee had been yesterday and nothing had intervened.

This is the kind of rain it's fun to watch from pubs and teashops, Rain, she says. She studies the raindrops trembling on his eyelids, remembering how his green eyes lit his face. A fey smile threatens his chiseled mouth.

Here is the boy Aisling Wynant instructed to rape her, the boy Aisling raped, the boy Aisling instructed her to rape. Rape, raping, raped, it feels like freezing rain, it freezes her tongue, instills in her a crippling stutter. And yet she's just delivered a lecture. She hadn't stuttered then, doesn't stutter now. She stutters under duress, Aisling Wynant duress.

This is the subject Sally Beaumont, Dr. Sally Beaumont, knows best. Her subject. Making statues speak. More properly, how ancient Egyptian priests said they made statues speak. How

117

ancient Egyptians believed it. Now, in Cambridge rain, Rain, Pip to the kids he'd defended against bullies with his baseball bat and his stony fists, splutters against his steely distrust of words, splutters the same way she stammers under duress.

You came here to what, Rain? To stare at me from an audience, not even to wave or nod, to leave without... without...

To spy, I came here to spy on you. To see if you're okay.

You know me in ways nobody else will ever know me, ways that make me shudder and tingle, and you came here to spy on me? Do I look okay to you?

Yes.

Christ, you're even more broken than I am. Well, that's that then, Sally, take care? What can that possibly mean? You fucked my ass in a barn window while lightning outside turned the world inside out and revealed its terrible creatures to us, and now you come here to say, Yes, I look okay, and that's it then?

He remembers her ecstatic mouth, never quite closed, hinting at some private rapture. The slight gap between her front teeth that had always seemed like a passcode.

They stare at each other, a red two-decker splashing them, until she notices a single tear streaking his face, casting a faery glint. He takes her face in his hands and kisses her, fey as mist. She steps back and smiles a smile that doubles back to Galilee, a wanton, precocious smile.

I know what you're thinking, Rain.

I know you do.

I'm sliding feet first into home plate. You look up my frock at my panties.

And you smile that smile. Yeah.

I'll never forget your look.

Died and gone to heaven.

Something like that... I'm not okay, not by a long shot. That's why you're here. That's what I choose to believe. Okay?

I was in a hospital getting over the latest goddam thing and I woke up staring at the night nurse's ass and thinking, knowing that the only thing I wanted was for you to be okay, otherwise nothing was going to be okay. Ever.

I think perhaps you heard my ex beating the piss out of me, leaving me standing in a puddle of my own pee in the middle of the night with my wrists tied around a stanchion. Well, not my ex yet, we're separated.

Would you like me to kill him, Sally?

That would be lovely, thank you. I know you could, Pip. I remember your berserker raids. So you'd have only half the story, and that wouldn't be enough to feast on. So can we get over this that's-that-then-thing and act like the… what, what are we, Pip? Each other's first love. We can't even say that, can we? You loved Dolores. D'you know that once, just once, I ran faster than Dolores? It was just after that night in the barn. Maybe I thought I had your permission. But we were each other's first lovers, weren't we? You know what I do for a living, if you can call it that? I'm an expert on how priests made those ancient Egyptian statues speak, or claimed to. More specifically, I'm an expert on the Colossi of Memnon at Luxor. Can you imagine that, the girl whose panties you can't forget…

Soiled panties, long golden legs, heavenly breath….

C'mon, let's get a drink.

I don't drink. Not anymore. Can't handle it.

Tea, let's get tea, let's… I don't know what the hell is happening. Isn't that a good feeling?

I always had, have a good feeling about you, Sally.

In the nearby Fairy Wren Tearoom he shakes the rain from his peacoat. Their conversation stalls. Her wrists are still tied around that post. She still stands shivering in her own pee. She feels on the verge of stammering. As usual, he's easy with silence. He reaches behind him and draws from his broad black belt a small sketchpad. He fetches a pencil from an inside pocket of his coat. He studies her as he always had, as if the earth will wobble in its orbit if he turns away. Then he begins to draw. Quickly. He makes three drawings of her, one a head only, another head and shoulders, and the third her profile, which he draws from memory. It seems as she watches him that he never lifts his hand from the page. He rips drawings from the spiral pad and hands them to her.

119

Pip, I'm not....

You are. That beautiful. Not pretty.

Don't you remember me as a tomboy?

He shakes his head: I remember you as lightning, thunder, electricity.

It thrills the Egyptologist in her. Doesn't this touch on the way the priests moved the colossi?

These are exquisite, Pip. I don't remember you drawing.

I didn't. I found I could one night in the ship's library in the Navy.

She hands them back.

His hands rest one on the other on the bare table. He shakes his head: They belong to you.

Belong, Pip?

Belong.

He doesn't belong. Sally belongs. In England, to England. But he belongs nowhere and longs to tell her but might well stutter himself.

She tries to remember that one thing that had always sent the current between them, bridged the silence. Then it arrives. Her boldness. Her fierce directness. If he hadn't loved her, he loved it. Sally could be counted on to say the one thing nobody wanted to hear. Nobody but Pip.

So I'm standing in my own pee with my wrists tied and my ass on fire. Because he's whipping me with his belt. And. . .

She looks into his eyes. It had always seemed to her as a girl she was going for a swim in them, those green eyes. Going naked.

And I'm thinking of you. I had been thinking of you. That was the problem, you see. He knew I was always thinking of someone else.

Keep on looking, Sally, don't turn away, don't look down, don't look past him, or you'll never be able to say it. It may be the thing that makes the statues move. Say it.

That was the problem, Pip. I was touching myself. He caught me. It made him crazy. He hurt me. I hurt. Masturbating, thinking about you. Like I always do. I'm stuck. Are you? Are you stuck, Pip?

How could she have said it. How, after coming back from Galilee to The Wash, to East Anglia, how after earning three degrees at Cambridge, could she possibly say such a thing to a Yank sailor, a stranger? But this is Rain, the only person on earth who isn't a stranger, for reasons neither of them had ever dared say.

Stuck. Yeah. The one thing I know about the girls and the women I've met is—they're not you. Not you, Sally. So that slams the door between them and me. Aisling's not you, either. She's there, but she's not you. That's all I know about them, no matter what they tell me, no matter what I learn, even if they look remotely like you. They're not you, you standing in the barn window, you hovering over me in Aisling's dressing room, us tutored by her, told what to do, in detail, shown what to do.

Touching myself, my pinky flying in the air, while you fucked my ass in a lightning storm. That's *there*, isn't it, Rain? The only *there* there really is. Masturbating, like the Viscount Abbott caught me, touching my *there*.

No.

No?

No. You've turned it around to hurt yourself. You're helping him, Sally. He didn't catch you. He profaned you. He came on a goddess performing her sacred rite, hers alone, the one assigned her by the gods, her absolute right, and Viscount Thug desecrated her, desecrated the moment she makes the world right again, the way she keeps the stars in their circuits, calms the storm.

Her mouth goes slack. She struggles to shut that ecstatic mouth he'd so finely drawn.

You're not mocking me, Rain. You….

I never mock anyone, Sally.

No, you don't. I remember. You listen to everyone, see everything. Everyone counts. But now you draw like Parmigianino and speak like, like… let me think, let me think. Like Rimbaud. Like *The Illuminations*.

That's our thing, Sally, the incomplete illuminations. That's why we're still standing in that window, facing north, Great South Bay behind, Daisy and Dolly whinnying, lightning cracking, thunder breaking, beasts disappearing in the bullbrier.

The incomplete illuminations. I don't ever want to be anywhere else. That's the beginning and the end of my life, alpha and omega. I don't want to be anywhere but here. Is this being stuck? I don't like being touched, Rain. I hardly like to touch myself. It doesn't feel like a sacred rite. It feels like a drat necessity, like squatting on the loo. I feel invaded whenever somebody stands too close. Everybody smells bad, harbors ill intent, looks too bright, too big. Does that ring any bells?

Whenever a woman begins to excite me I know the circuit is going to burn out, I smell acrid wiring, I know the current is going to fizzle. I just want to get away and think of you and the time when that fierce circuit could be trusted. But I never wanted to come find you because you'd be in love and married, you'd be upset to see me, I'd intrude, we wouldn't like each other, or some damned thing. So I'm stuck. And, and everything that happens, it happens in Aisling's shadow, in her giant shadow, under her perfect tits. Everything smells like Aisling, looks like Aisling, everything except you. That's what the barn window is about. It wasn't Aisling's bedroom, her bathroom, her dressing table, her bed. It was us. For a moment we were free. But we couldn't grow up. We couldn't do anything about that one moment. We couldn't get out of it, we couldn't go on, we only pretended to go on. We sent our facsimiles on.

That one moment like Bernini's *Ecstasy of Saint Catherine*. And then we pretended to live someone else's life.

Yes. Like that. What the hell is the epilogue for that?

What if I knew? What if you came to Cambridge because I know? Would that be any more magical than that moment? It transfigured us. Didn't it? Do you remember how we looked at each other after that? Me with my mere hints of tits, you with that crazy look you got at home plate?

Yeah, like we had seen God. Like words were just too filthy to speak. Like, well, that's it then, what else could possibly be better? We'd have to be greedy to look for more.

Had we? Seen God? Did we look for more? You said Viscount Thug profaned a goddess. Why did that come to your mind? How did that come out of your mouth, Rain, that mouth so reluctant to say anything at all? You were never eloquent. Where do you get off being eloquent now?

It was that word, *caught*. You said he caught you. It pissed me off. You were helping your enemy. Looking up to the bastard. You should be looking down on him. He doesn't even deserve you to piss on him.

So now to go on, to stop pretending, to make the colossi speak, make Aisling speak. We couldn't know how each of us would look or talk, could we? But here we are, and I'm not stammering. Here we are, Egyptologist and sailor. Let's imagine how we might speak. Let's move the colossi. Let's listen.

How do you know I'm a sailor? My peacoat?

I'm a good spy, too. I keep track of you as best I can. Afraid for the same reasons to find you. What else did I have to hold on to? Why would I spoil it? Without it I might not survive at all. That's the risk you took coming here. That's why you walked away, not to spoil it. That's the risk I took running into the street after you. Maybe Aisling ruined us, but maybe she gave us to each other, too. Maybe there's something in that evil, her evil, we need for our elixir, the thing we need to ennoble base elements. Maybe Aisling did evil without being evil. Maybe evil is necessary to transfigure us.

He shook his head slowly.

I, I have something. I've been drawing Aisling. Not you, just Aisling. I don't know why. Lots of drawings. Too many to count. I think it's why I started to draw. And then one night, in the middle of the night, I had this dream. A crocodile was lying on top of me and I couldn't breathe, couldn't move. Help, I said, help me, and some kid, none of the kids we knew at Galiliee, came into the room where this crocodile was lying on top of me in bed. The kid was frail and confused, and I knew he couldn't help me. But he tried. Then I woke up. It was almost dawn. I heard a few horns, a truck beeping as it backed up—and Aisling. I heard Aisling. She started to talk. You know, that hoarse, Scouse accent of hers. I started scribbling it all down, and when she'd stop I drew her. They're so erotic, these drawings, I can smell her, so I wouldn't show them to anyone. They're creatures of my painfully eidetic memory.

But me. You'd show them to me, because I remember that Scouse accent, her smell. I remember, Pip. How couldn't I?

Yeah, of course.

I played a lot of baseball after you went home to England. I hardly ever saw anybody running the third base line without thinking about you. I played for the Saint Joseph's team, can you believe that? The priests called me their little heretic.

The rain turns hard and races at an angle across the tea shop's window, reminding them both of the barn window that night.

I was wearing a frock—that's what we called them then— because our uniforms were in the laundry. It was breezy. I saw the dust swirling around you. I was going to knock the ball out of your hand. I smile when I think of your flabbergasted face. Nobody since has ever been quite so taken by me. You hardly ever talked, Pip. And I wondered if after that collision at home plate you ever would again.

We didn't talk much after, you know, Aisling … and I think the cordgrass had something to do with it. It was always saying shush, shush.

Yeah, I know. And we listened. But we walked a lot in the wash in the cordgrass and held hands a lot. And now that I think of it that was quaint. I mean, maybe Victorian kids did that, but kids in West Islip in the forties? I wake up in the morning quite often seeing us walking in the cordgrass. The sun is always coming up over our left shoulders, coming up wrong. I'm an Egyptologist, the sun can't come up wrong. I see us from behind. It's a waking dream, the dream that wakes me, that holds off the day. You're wearing that windbreaker with all the insignias on it, even the silver breast eagle the Afrika Korps POWs gave you. You meant something to them. Not because you spoke some baby German but because you seemed a prisoner to them, too. I'm wearing a frock with a blue sweater. I think it's autumn. We're facing the bay, Great South Bay, where everything happened and would happen if only we could figure it out, make *Ludilon* whole again, sail away. I can still smell it. I was born on The Wash of East Anglia, Pip, but it's Great South Bay I smell. I don't think we've ever let go of each other's hand, have we? Or found the words to talk about what happened. We weren't ready, weren't ready for any of it. You had Dolores to talk to, you always had Dolores. She set tea places in that crumbling gazebo, imaginary tea in painted tin cups, and you sat with her for what seemed like hours, talking. What did you talk about, Pip? You loved each other. What did you talk about? Did you talk or did the rest of us just imagine it, and why was it important to us that you two sit there and sip air tea?

But after… after Aisling, the barn, I didn't have Dolores, Sally. I had….

Me. In the barn. In Aisling's rooms, in the cordgrass, in *Ludilon*. Me, you had me, and I had you. And, damn it, we have to know why. Dolores had long legs, too, Pip. Truth is, she ran faster than me. The only thing she didn't do better than me was blonde, she didn't do blonde better than me. You loved her. I hated it. I hated that you loved her. And then she was gone. First loves are usually not the ones we end up with, are they? She lost what I had. What I had from you. But I never had what she had from you. Pure beyond reach. I excited you. I twisted you. But Dolores had Pip before the blood storm. And she always will.

Puberty, you mean?

And Aisling. Puberty and Aisling. What did they call you later, Pip, after Galilee?

Bo.

Beau? Beauregard. Beaumont, as in my family?

No. B-o. Bo, for boatswain, as in boatswain's mate. I joined the Merchant Marine and then the Navy. I struck for a boatswain's rating, and guys called me Bo. It was okay, so it stuck. Or sometimes Boats.

Bo. Okay, I like it. So I won't call you Rain anymore. Or Pip.

You can call me anything you want, Sally Beaumont. You can call me a son of a bitch, a bastard. Actually, I'm both. You….

Bo, I'm going to call you Bo, Bo of the cordgrass, Bo of the barn, home plate, *Ludilon* Bo, flabbergasted Bo, silent Bo, berserker Bo.

Bo of the cordgrass, I like that, Sally.

That's what I think of when I wake up. That's what I think when I know I'm going to stammer. You didn't even notice I stammer because I don't with you. What didn't I notice, Bo?

He turns from her face to the rainy window. Suddenly, suddenly, Sally, we knew....

Suddenly Sally! Oh, I like that very much, Bo. I'm your Sudden Sally, aren't I?

I was going to say, I'm trying to say we suddenly knew too much about each other, more than we could grasp. But we didn't know enough, either. It didn't even occur to me what Aisling might have done to you alone. Or to the others. Did such things occur to you, Sally?

No. Just what was happening to us. Everything I recognized about it was too late, much too late. And all I've salvaged out of it is you. I don't know how to be unhappy about you. Do you know how to be unhappy about me?

No. I can't imagine anything, anyone, not having known you first. I try. I, I can't. I can't imagine a world that doesn't hinge on you being in it. I see now that's why I came here.

And walked away?

Scared.

You were never scared of much, not that I could tell.

Scared, Sally. Scared you'd have a husband, kids, a loving family, no room for me, no room for me for a minute, an entire England where I don't belong. You'd...

You should shut up, Bo. Shut up. Your perfect antennae felt their way here. And everything you feared is wrong, and maybe that's what you really feared. Is it? Could that be possible?

Now she dives head first into that quarry, that green quarry, Bo's eyes.

It's what I feared, Bo. Wanted. Feared and wanted. That there'd be room for me.

He leans back with both hands on the table.

Do you think of the cordgrass, of holding my hand?

Of not saying anything, not having to say anything, not having anything to say, being afraid to say anything. Two people who didn't need words. And now we do, as if we've regressed.

Yeah. I do. How the sun lit your hair. How you smelled. How you were always going to give me that crazy grin and I was always not going to know what to do.

And at that point, Bo, you knew a lot about how I smelled, how I tasted, more, really, than anybody else has ever known, more than I want anybody else to know. The thing is if I wasn't going to want anybody else to know such things, to know me, then you couldn't exist either, and as long as you did you were a big problem. Am I your big problem?

No. I'm still holding your hand. I need you to exist. You're my first intimacy. My only intimacy. I know you gave a damn once like nobody else ever did or ever has. You gave a damn when you didn't even know how. I was afraid to come here for a lot of reasons I didn't think I'd be able to get out of my mouth. I thought I'd be like I was after Aisling. Frozen. Locked up. Shut down. I had the drawings, I had what Aisling said, what I imagined her saying. I didn't know what you'd think. But I had an argument with myself. If you're afraid of Sally, who wouldn't you be afraid of?

Who won this argument, Bo?

This halfling, this bastard stranger who kills people instead of making love, because he's a sexual short-circuit. His current is always, almost always, diverted at the moment of contact, so he kills people to compensate. So was I supposed to come tell you this, as if it was your problem?

It is my problem, Bo. So you decided to just come and spy? Something perhaps we both learned from Aisling, don't you think? And now you've said it. And I've said it. Damaged goods. Walking dead. Zombies. Aisling's zombies. That's what we are. Could it possibly have been any other way? And is there anybody else in the world who could possibly understand the way we do?

Except, we don't, do we, Sally? I mean, yeah, we know a lot, we've just told each other a lot, we've both figured out things on our own, but what do we really know?

I'm a scholar, you're a sailor. I looked happy to you. You didn't look happy to me. I figured you out, I drew you out. I ran after you. But you did come a long way to reach a bum conclusion about me, Bo, and that's a start, isn't it? What do they call it, that thing you're in? Black ops, am I right? Well, Jesus Christ, Bo, we're victims of black ops, aren't we? We know a lot about black ops.

We know you don't have to kill people to ruin them. Aisling made us excess, surplus. What did we make her? We can maybe know what we make of her, but can we ever know what we made her?

But are we ruined, Bo? Are we? We're twisted, we're bent, burnt, harmed, but are we ruined? Did we think we'd be here behind a rainy window in this teashop saying things we never thought we could say, me not stammering, you not looking away? I want to see those drawings, I want to hear what Aisling said. I'll tell you what I said after the war, after I went home. I'll tell you what Sally still says sliding into home plate. I'll let you see those panties again, Bo. But I want something big, something tremendous from you. I want you to be my colossus, I want to animate you, I want you to say what I can't stammer out of me, say it to my enemies, my blood enemies. I want you to kill them for me.

Kill?

Not so they'll be blood to wash off your hands, but so their mirrors will mock them, so they'll know the exact moment they died, so they'll know they're only playing at life. Kill them that way, Bo. For me. Don't make me say the words. Let them animate you. Listen like we listened to each other in the wash, holding hands, looking out on the bay, not knowing what to say and saying more than we would ever say to anyone else. That was our triumph, the moment of our transfiguration, the moment we became what we are. We didn't disgust each other. We didn't deny each other. We didn't renounce each other. We held hands. Think, what a marvelous thing that was. That's when we inhabited ourselves. Left alone, if you hadn't come here, maybe we would have gone on thinking ourselves disembodied, thinking Aisling disembodied us, made it impossible to inhabit ourselves, our bodies. That's how I felt. I don't know about you, of course I don't. What do you think? I wrote all my theses, my doctoral papers, standing in the cordgrass with you, holding your hand. Standing in that window in that big, eerie Victorian barn with its turrets and slate roofs, its stalls, its servants' quarters, Daisy and Dolly, my pinky fluttering in the lightning flashes, you galvanizing me. My disembodied self. My Aisling self could never have gone on, never written those papers, gotten those degrees. But holding hands with you in the cordgrass, two of us walking dead, that way I could do it.

• • •

This candor, is it more than he bargained for? Or is it what he'd come for? Too much of a good thing? Honesty he has, candor's another thing. He doesn't lie to anyone, and he tries not to lie to himself, a trickier proposition. His pal, Terry Mabry, said to him more than once, Ya just had to say that, didn't ya, Bo? But that isn't quite Sally Beaumont's gig. Her gig is saying what's sure to give you the shivers, what's sure to rattle you, the one dread thing you spent your life trying not to hear. A dark angel's about to speak.

As if she hears him think, she speaks over the plashing rain.

Remember Billy Kilgore, Bo?

Not Alan Banks, the upperclassman who raped him, but Billy Kilgore, his first roommate, bully, thief, liar, slob. A loathsome creep who'd terrorized him until one day in the middle of the nightmare that was Galilee he realized he'd grown bigger and stronger than Billy.

You! You were drying dishes in the pantry. Barbara was washing them. I passed through with my baseball bat. You saw blood in my eye. How did you know, Sally? How did you know where I was going? What I was going to do? Kill him, you said. No exclamation mark. No expression on your face. Kill him, you said. Matter of fact, like I should, like I might, like I would. Barbara said nothing. As if I was going to play baseball after dark. But you knew exactly where I was headed, and you had no clue, none. You just knew.

And you damned near did. Kill him. I'll bet his head never worked right again, not that it ever did. Everybody knew. It swept through Galilee like crown fire. And after that, after that you were Spartacus. Anybody hanging around you was probably being intimidated by someone. You were refuge.

You said kill him, and Barbara didn't even put her dish down. You changed my life. I've spent my life killing him, killing Billy Kilgore. Alan Banks, Billy Kilgore, Aisling Wynant, yeah, they changed me, but you stone-cold told me to kill Billy, like you knew something about me I didn't know. And somehow, I don't know how, that's how we ended up in Aisling's bedroom, us two deadly kids, that's how we became two dead kids in Galilee, Aisling Wynant's golems, made of her bad parts and the other junk in that yard. Mud struck with lightning, the two of us... Goddammit to hell, why did you say that, Sally?

Because I thought it would be a good idea.

To say it?

To kill him. Somebody had to kill him. It seemed right to me it should be you.

Jesus Christ, Sally.

I don't think he had much to do with it. Remember that big banner in Gothic letters in Sunday School that said, Suffer the little children to come unto me? Well, they didn't, and they sure as hell suffered. They came unto Aisling, she killed the little bastards. She suffered them. They suffered her. But Jesus, he was out to lunch.

Bo smiles in spite of himself. Sally talks, she doesn't stammer with him, she talks like that wanton grin she gave him when he looked up her frock at home plate. That was the real Sally, the one Aisling gave him instead of Dolores, instead of Barbara.

Did she?

Did she what, Bo?

I was wondering if Aisling gave me you, or was it in the pantry that night or later at home plate?

Well, let's not credit her with the wrong thing. Nobody could have engineered that incredibly flummoxed look on your face.

Or your dirty grin.

Or my very clear instruction to you in the pantry. Nobody. You were in love with Dolores, you had a flustered crush on my sister because she touched your arm when you passed each other, but I had my eye on you, and put together we added up.

Put together?

Mmm, al Jabara, the joining, Algebra, letters standing for numbers.

Yeah, but get this, Sally, the original meaning of al Jabara is the joining of broken parts. So it's the putting together *again.*

As in broken before Aisling the Algebraist made our letters stand for numbers. But what letters, what numbers? Could I have been the letter A, its pinnacle my little crotch? Could you have been the letter V as in lightning bolt?

Or a hyphen or a dash? Or... what could we have been, Sally? Each other's broken parts?

Well, I spend my life deciphering such matters, Bo. I read hieroglyphs, I imagine monuments and statues speaking, I write their scripts in search of answers. Hey, d'you know why you have a raptor's face, a Horus face?

Bo's cheeks ripple, hinting a smile.

To keep the light of your eyes from holding hands. The green light. To keep you focused, like a raptor.

Seconds pass.

That's how you looked at me when I said, Kill him. Like you were about to smile. That's....

How you know I like you?

Yes. You don't smile. It's not in your job description. Talking is not even in your job description. But I make you smile because you know I'm a fellow berserker. Even if now I stammer. I'm a stammering berserker. Sally the Stammerer.

A lightning bolt strikes the lamppost, races down its stem and splits it open. A wire thrashes back and forth in the street, sparking in the splattering rain.

Their faces drain, their eyes meet like naked children in a cold attic. They're thinking—and they know they're thinking—of the barn window, the crazy intercourse of desperate, blundering children. But what Sally doesn't know is that he's thinking of what she'd said about animating the colossi.

What is Horus thinking?

131

I dunno, do gods think one thing at a time?

You know a lot about lightning rods, don't you, Horus? Being one yourself, I mean. I know ships have them. I heard it mentioned in connection with Saint Elmo's Fire.

Green flash. Yeah.

Like your face, Horus. They install lightning rods to protect the colossi and such like. D'you think it's possible one of us called down that lightning bolt?

Or two of us?

Two of us together. Two kids from Galilee. Aisling's walking dead holding hands, screwing each other silly in a moldy barn in a thunderstorm, being screwed, screwed up, and suddenly powerful as hell for all the wrong reasons, grown up, burned out, robbed, cheated, their third eyes wide open and staring, staring now into each other, summoning, conjuring.

I'm staying at the Longboat. It's only two blocks from here.

Not far from Galilee either, is it, Bo?

Nothing ever is.

• • •

Night spent at the barn window, lightning crackling inside and out, shatters them. Morning is square one. Morning is mourning. Morning strange and frightening. A young woman loath to be touched, sometimes finding it difficult to touch herself, and a killing man, broken, burned, acrid, each of them now in possession of something thought irretrievable last night, each of them stricken with an old power over each other, each of them aware of someone absent, Aisling Wynant, orchestrator, choreographer, conjuror, evildoer.

God help us, each of them wants to say. But what to say, after she uses his spare toothbrush, after pulling up the panties she'd washed out the night before, after they shower, after shattering each other again, what to say? Nothing, not while the sun needles the blinds, somehow threateningly. They hold hands, as they had in the cordgrass, as they had on the beach gazing at *Ludilon*. Sally gets up first. Bo's afraid to look. She walks to the bathroom slowly, wanting him to look, and when he does his eyes sting. The loo croaks. She comes back into the room naked, her panties dangling from her long fingers, giving him that home plate leer.

Sally, I, I have an idea.

Better than the one you had last night?

Uh, different.

I can't deal with them on an empty stomach, Pip.

Them?

Mmm, them ideas.

• • •

Sometimes you can draw things out of a drawing you can't draw out of your head. That's how I started drawing. I was doodling. Abstract stuff, maybe a little like Kandinsky. I didn't know I could draw an object, a person. Then one day I drew Aisling. Just like that.

They stand on Clare Bridge looking down at a River Cam crumpled by a brisk breeze, a breeze he thinks might carry his words away before they reach Sally's ear. He shifts position downwind to upwind.

There you are! she cries.

It wasn't just like that, Sally. It was Aisling's....

Cunt! Cunt, she says, grinning.

You think it's funny?

I think you're funny. We know a lot about the subject at hand, Bo. Don't we. You drew Aisling's cunt. Tell me yours, I'll tell you mine.

Like a wet weed in the morning. Pearly drops hanging from milkweed turning brown with this faint pink wound running down the middle. I looked at my hand, my left hand. I thought it was someone else's, someone who could draw like this.

You're right-handed. I remember.

No, I was always a lefty, and when I left home, if that's what you could call that fen, I decided to undo, to try to undo what people had forced me to do. I don't believe my right hand would ever have drawn Aisling, or anything else. It was that one thing that helped me go on, that helped me survive. Going back to being a lefty, my side sinister, symbol of bastardy. You wouldn't think that one thing helped me salvage myself, but it did.

Aisling's cunt. What did you do about the fragrance?

You're into this, aren't you, Sally?

In for a penny....

Well, it was right there in the drawing, her fragrance, and it all scared the crap out of me. I kept on looking at my left hand. Okay, I said finally, tell me what you want to say, what I don't want to hear, go on, tell me, I'm listening, I'm looking. And it did. My left hand did. I made dozens of drawings of Aisling, the things she did, to herself, not to us. I left us out. It was important to leave us out. We'd gone on, to the fen, holding hands, hanging out on *Ludilon*.

• • •

Sally's ecstatic mouth is wet, the slight gap between her front teeth a gate swung open. He has the thought, the vulgar thought, to check her panties, to see if they're moist, and she looks at him as if she knows it.

They're, they're erotic in ways I'm not, or didn't know I was, obscene. They're so goddamned inappropriate I figured after a while they must be the most appropriate thing in my life, otherwise, how could I do them so well? Even I knew how good they were. And I knew my right hand, my taught hand, the hand others taught, couldn't have made them.

You're going to tell me you destroyed them, you didn't, did you, Bo?

I thought about it. Who the hell was I going to show them to? I figured they might be like the picture of Dorian Gray in the attic.

Are they?

I don't know. Maybe. They're as horrid, as hot, as frightening as she was. And we're not in them, but we're there, Sally, in the corner, in the bed, in the bathroom, we're there, two kids about to die with only the faintest inkling of what to do about the itch, what to do about your long legs, your panties, your hot face, my fixed eyes, my berserker sorties, my flummoxed face when I looked at you. We're there, like paint, like dust, like light, necessary, unseen.

And all that's to come, what we sense, my stammer, your....

See, I have this idea. I give you these drawings. I even give you some scraps of poems I've written about what happened in Galilee. We go away, Sally. We don't stay. Not now. Because otherwise we just stay in that window, otherwise we're stuck.

But I want to stay in that window, Bo.

I do too, but we don't grow up in that window, we don't go on, we don't become anything more than we were. I need to sell this idea to you. You take the drawings. You study them. You can even destroy them. Or make paper boats out of them and sail them here on River Cam, anything you want. Read my scraps of shit. Then you send me whatever you think, whatever you can see, with your stammer even. So that way we know a little more about us after we couldn't get back to that window.

Like we just did, you mean?

Yeah, but after all this time. Here's what I'm trying to tell you—and please believe I didn't have a plan when I came here, I wasn't even thinking about the drawings—at some point, I was in the North Sea in a gale, sailing on an old course, because I couldn't get a star fix, and I realized that Aisling's cunt, Aisling really, is a black hole, and the galaxy—you and I would never call it the heavens, would we?—is disappearing into that black hole, that fragrant black hole. We're disappearing, everything we know is disappearing, everything we trusted, all the familiar constellations, all being drawn out and sucked in. Goodbye Barbara, goodbye Dolores, goodbye what was left to reassure us. And once I knew that, once I saw that, well, it was the beginning of seeing that I'd have to know how you were to keep on living. But I never thought, I never planned, until last night, that the three of us, me, you and Aisling, could figure it all out together, and now I do. I think maybe we can.

But how to make Aisling speak, how to move that statue? How to conjure lightning—do the scariest, most contrary thing? What rituals?

I'm suggesting a ritual, Sally. And lightning, well, it struck the lamppost last night, didn't it? I've tried. I've put words in Aisling's mouth, Sally. You remember how she sounded, right. She whispered, and we couldn't figure out how someone who whispered like an angel in our ears would do the things we were doing, the things she was doing, and we couldn't even figure out if we were lucky or gone to hell-and-gone, could we? But when I started to put words in her mouth she started to put her fingers across my mouth to shut it so she could speak, like her wet fingers, remember?

I remember. Wet, forbidden, exciting, scary, I remember.

Paper boats in the Cam? And you wouldn't be angry?

No. There would be a reason. It would be a good reason. You don't have any bad reasons where I'm concerned.

And you don't where I'm concerned, Bo. That's something, really something to know, isn't it?

He nods.

So Aisling, she's not a banshee, not a she-devil?

Yes, she is, Sally. There was a death in our house. She killed us. We saw it coming. She came home, boozy, blowsy, beautiful, way too fragrant. Home? I mean Galilee, upstream from the Dead Sea, the rest of our lives. After Aisling we were the walking dead. We are the walking dead. But I'm saying we can give her the power to resurrect us. She is a Sidhe, a faery woman. That's where the word banshee comes from. We have to consent to shudder, to shiver in her presence, like we did. If I haven't made the sale, Sally, let me try one more pitch. I know I'm proposing what could be the death of us, but Aisling is the death of us, so in a sense we've nothing to lose.

Stop. I'm going to do it, Bo. You've made the sale. It appeals to my specialty, making the colossus speak, but mostly it appeals to my sense of the undone, the unapprehended.

The undead?

Yes, the undead who bathe in the Dead Sea and drink its salt water. But go ahead and make your pitch, because what else is a morning watching the River Cam good for but seeing where thoughts we think in Cambridge go?

It's about what didn't happen last night. It's about what I didn't even fear would happen last night. I live like a knight templar, but not because of any vow. I don't do sex because I know something deep inside me is shorted and burned out. I know that no matter how excited I get it won't last long enough to do anybody any good because it disappears, fizzling into that black hole. Fear comes shooting down my wiring, it hits something gone awry, something cut and hanging loose, and shorts out. As if Aisling had made a eunuch of me.

Stop! Stop, Bo. At this moment we may as well be androgynes. I know what happened to you, because I've been faking being a woman ever since. I don't know what I am, but it's not what society says I ought to be. Maybe I'm not whole, or maybe I'm whole in a way I can't explain to anyone but you, and only because you dared tell me what happened to you, what really happened. I'd say it's as if she performed a clitoridectomy on me, but that's too facile. If Onan hadn't been a man I'd say Aisling made an onanist of me, had limited me to the circumnavigation of a pond, an endangered pond. And last night a templar stood in the Longboat and re-enacted a scene from our ripped-up childhood, a scene that transcended our wounds, our disabilities, and now we're standing on Clare Bridge, rain gathering again, contemplating a terrible adventure in search of the banshee who killed us. Have I got that right?

He starts to nod but thinks better of it. No.

No?

No, Sally. Maybe this is something you have to say on a bridge, something like a bridge. I mean, I want to say, I want to say I don't know what women need men for. I don't know why a goddess wouldn't prefer her own touch. It's the way she reorders, repairs, restores her part of the cosmos, it's the way she calls it back to order, and I think maybe that's what Aisling was doing, and we were handy. Recruited. Not the perfect instruments, but new and easy to master. I think we looked as if we needed to be used, and it would be a pity not to use us, a kind of sacrilege even.

So we can't go walking hand in hand in the cordgrass, we can't stand in the barn window, taking part in the electrification of the world, being electrocuted.

I'm not saying that, Sally, I'm just saying we ought to collect what we've become and see how much of it we can hand over to each other, how much we can tell about ourselves without getting in our own way. Because we'll get in each other's way, because we'll get in our own ways. I know this from long hours at sea. Two's a crowd. Sometimes one's a crowd. We've got to get out of our own way. It's not goodbye, it's like planning a rendezvous at the exact moment when the two of us can do more than each of us alone. We have to encounter Aisling alone. The drawings, my left hand, taught me that, my bastardy taught me that. But maybe like two stones we can only strike fire together.

You know, Bo, of course, each of us did encounter her alone, and we've never talked about it, right? I mean, in a sense, we're Aisling's children, incestuous children.

I do know. Yes. I know because I know it wasn't you who shorted me out, you're not the black hole into which my childhood and my future disappeared. Yes, I shivered at the thought of you, but that was because I had discovered the forbidden. You and Aisling were two kinds of forbidden. There was a coming back from you. There always would be. I trusted you. You liked me, you wished me no harm. Aisling was beyond trust, beyond wishing harm. No walking back from her. I knew that. You were Sally whose pigtails I longed to tie and untie, whose legs dazzled me. But Aisling knew something in me, something dark. She had something on me, or so I thought. She had me in her pocket. She could unravel me.

I thought it too. She knew I wasn't the little girl I pretended to be. I wasn't Sally Beaumont, I was a succubus. She had inside information. We were outsiders. We had to go along or else. She had the power to pick the fruit, we didn't. She had the reach. She had the authority. We didn't know how to do anything except shiver and shudder.

Which we did a lot, I remember. Once we exchanged those looks at home plate.

She kisses him feyly. The Cam quickens. The Cam carries their words downstream.

• • •

Dear Bo,

Your drawings of Aisling, your mad drawings, are like standing in the barn window. Sometimes I think I'm looking at me. If they weren't so exquisitely executed I'd have written sooner. How long has it been? Three months since our night in the Longboat, since we stood on Clare Bridge and made this pact. I've had them on the dining room table, on my lap, in my bed, on the coffee table, in my briefcase. I've traced every line with my fingertips. I've fondled our nemesis, Bo, sometimes fondly, sometimes with dread. There she is standing with one finger up her ass and the other twiddling her cunt, her pinky flagging the air, signaling, just like mine. Signaling what? We remember that, don't we? We remember what's coming. She brushes her long wet fingers across our lips, she guides you up her buttered ass. I'm so angry, Bo, so excited, so out of myself. Paralyzed. Are you? Paralyzed. I don't know how many days passed before I wrote this poem. I don't know, is it a poem, what is it? It's a circuit-breaker. I fear it's going to break our circuit, but I had to write it, and I have to send it to you. That's our pact. We must be brave enough to keep it or we're nothing. Our lives depend on it. No therapist is going to pull us out of this black hole. I think somehow you knew that when you decided so improbably to come here. Here it is, Bo. Not Sally suddenly. Not Sally lasciviously. Not Sally wantonly. Do you know this Sally, will you know this Sally? Will you even want to?

I don't want to be someone's receptacle,
an ATM, container, vessel, means. Do you
want to be a prod, rod, god, poker, sapper?
The idea of being human's vulgar,
at best a chrysalis, a waiting
for the worst to be over, and when
it's made important, when it struts
it gets in the way of itself, we trip
over each other, we push each other aside

en route to God-knows-where
as if God were anything but all,
anything other than all, a convenience.
No, I'm not open to your deposits,
your insertions, what you're banking on.
Say you won't be my diddler, give me
a reason to trust you other than frottage,
something deviant and holy like a drawing.
Sally

Dear Sally,

That's the keystone drawing. Maybe you notice it's just a few continuous lines. That's because it came in what seemed like an instant. I had no photographs of Aisling. It's entirely from memory. In fact, it's how I learned I could draw from memory. This tall, beautiful woman contorted, in a way—I think it's an unmistakable way—that tells you hell is breaking loose. But here's the damndest thing, when I asked myself what this drawing means—and that's something artists hate to do, and hate you to do—one word came to mind. Just one word. Betrayal. This is a picture of betrayal. I hated the word. It's so moralistic, preachy. But, like the drawing, the word opened Aisling to me in a way she never opened herself, even though she opened far too much of herself to us. I knew it meant she betrayed herself as well as us. I knew she had opened the gates of hell to herself as well as to us. The other drawings, her misty bush, her startled nipples, her dazed look, they don't convey this twistedness, this invitation. But invitation to what? Could it be—I'm dying to see your face right now—could it be she was teaching us how to keep the stars in their courses, how to keep the world from falling apart? Millions of people were killing each other. The Nazis were running death factories. Aisling had lost her husband. All us kids were alone and frightened, torn from home, bewildered. Did you ever talk to your sister Barbara about any of this? It's easy to think Aisling preyed on others. But suppose she didn't? We don't know. We'll never know. Some shrinks would say we can be pretty damn sure she did, but my own shrink told me it was no comfort at all to assume she was a serial predator. Aisling pulled off a crime. Against us. Did she repeat it? Were we repeats? We don't know. We're not looking to start an Aisling Survivors Club, after all.

Here's another drawing. I'm not in it, but I'm over to the right out of sight on her bed. She's sitting at her dressing table. I remember the way the evening light from the window played on her legs. I had scarlet fever. I was burning up. There was snow on the ground and the night before, I ran outside in my pajamas and bare feet and dived head first into a snowbank. We were Christian Scientists, so I was sweating it out. There she is, pointing with her beautiful finger at her cunt. Her hands were a work of art, remember? And I'm there out of view, knowing what to do, dreading it, enthralled by it, scared, and, now I realize, angry. Yeah, the kid is angry. But what's he going to do, pick up his baseball bat and bop her, like he did Billy Kilgore? He doesn't want to do it, he wants to do it, he wants to be far away, he wants to sail *Ludilon* away, but everything is lost to him, to Sally. His grandma Huldah, his aunt Dorothy, his nanny Peggy, everyone he counted on, gone. And there he is in that heady bed with this giantess telling him what she wants him to do. She was tall, wasn't she, Sally? Tall… I've got to go. Some emergency. Icebergs, maybe.

Your old chum,

Bo

Dear Bo,

Not as tall as we are. But in our minds she'll always loom over us. There will never be enough light in her shadow. She can't be reduced to size. She can't be retouched, flipped, cropped like a photo.

Was it a ship's emergency, or something you invented because you couldn't go on? I would understand. Maybe it was just Aisling looking over your shoulder, whispering in your ear. I would understand. I remember what she called me, the words she used to describe me. Exquisite. Perfect. Morning glory. Her little honeysuckle. Trouble is when I look at my ass in the mirror it's Aisling's ass. Not hers to wear, but hers to own. It belongs to her because of what she did with it. I can't get it back. I can't even cover it properly. Can you imagine that? I can't cover my ass, no matter how much money I spend on it. No matter what I wear. I can't go on right now, but I had to say this right away. Because of Aisling I'm always naked and over-dressed to hide it. And this: Maybe we own parts of her as much as she owns parts of us.

One other thing. We're making the colossi speak. Don't you think?

Well, two other things. Are you hot for me? Now? When you read my letters? I am for you. What is that? Good or bad? We've been missing each other since I slid into home plate, since Aisling, since we walked in the cordgrass and I started to stammer, but never with you. So why aren't we more, I don't know what, more functional? Or are we as functional as we'll ever be? And could we be more functional with other people? Or less? I've tried. I'm sure you have. Couldn't get it over with quick enough. Hate someone fiddling with me, tinkering with me, playing with me, playing me. Hate it.

Feet first on the third base line,
Sally

Dear Sally,

Hard as we try to be honest, I think we reinvent the past. There's a sailor's term: marlinspike. It can be used to describe the spike sailors use to untie a knot, and it can be used to describe the whole range of sailor's skills. I think a memory is a knot. We can untie it, but it will never be quite the same. The fiber will have worn away, the rope will have a shape of its own, rot will have set in, oils will have soaked in, and even when the knot is retied the exact same way it will be different. We can call it a bowline, but it won't be the same bowline. And that's assuming honest intent. After that, there's the danger of rejiggering everything. Or maybe it's like the four gospels—which one is the most accurate? And does accurate mean a recital of facts or a search for their underlying meaning or revelation incited by an event?

Yeah, I know, I'm equivocating. I am. I don't trust myself to tell the truth. I trust you. But me, I'm bent, crazed, cross-eyed with anger and confusion. Truth? Let me ramble, sneak up on your question. A while back my mother was trying to con me into signing a waiver that would give her complete control of my stepfather Dominick's estate. I was going to sign it anyway, but she was worried I wouldn't, because in my shoes she wouldn't. We're sitting in this genteel lawyer's office, just the three of us, and he says at some point, The truth is… and she throws a glass paperweight at him and shouts, The truth? The truth is what I goddamn well say it is. First things first: she missed him, thank God. I signed the waiver and walked out. Haven't seen her since. But I remember what she said, and I'm afraid of it. I don't want the truth to be what I say it is, not about Aisling, not about you or me. But here's the thing, Sally: the bare facts, even if we agree on them, won't tell us what we're looking for. So I'm stuck. For the moment. But I'll keep on thinking and write when I have something to say, something I trust. The truth always seems to me bent by the time it took getting back to us.

Your question. Yeah, others, there have been others, and sometimes you might say we had sex, if you can say sex is getting each other off, but most of the time the only thing reliable about me is two feet walking out the door in the middle of the night. Most of the time I'm not there. You're not there. The barn's not there. And if I can't turn someone into you or Aisling I'm just a wet noodle.

Oh, one other thing. I have a name for Aisling. Ravishing Do-Gooder. Here's a scrap of a poem I made:

Ravishing do-gooder
When I see a storm system saddle the mountains
I'm as set as a mustang to throw riders off.

It's the blanket that's going to smother me
pretending to mother me, drunken caretaker
yammering to me about my own good.
When I see a storm taking up residence
I think of a rapist's close breath, I think
of my impending death. Then lightning cracks
and I see in the clearing creatures that might be
angels as well as demons, hope not for respite
but strength to trample the ravishing do-gooder.
Bo

Bo, if you've learned to lie, it was after I left Galilee. Barbara and I both worried about you not being able to lie. We regarded it as necessary gear. It excited us that you couldn't, but we liked you and foresaw calamity. We thought it was going to get you killed, and it almost did, as I'm sure you remember, when bullies tried to hang you from the hay trolley and Henry McKee from next door rescued you.

The facts are already bare and bared, Bo. We agree on them.

It doesn't surprise me you'd grow up to be a sailor, but an artist and a poet—well, it frightens me. Take your ravishing do-gooder, your Medea of the misty bun, we could spend a lifetime on her anatomy. I don't know what I expected you to be, Bo. I expected you to be Pip, not Bo. And, Bo, I think, I guess I didn't give Pip much of a chance of surviving. I just didn't know your expiration date, and I think Barbara, more than me, feared it was close. I… I'm stammering here on the loo writing to you while my bath pours, stammering in the altogether. You always did bring up the damnedest subjects, I remember that. It made Barbara laugh, not that she'd ever tell you, but it did something else to me. It made me jumpy, as I was in the barn window, as you made me, impaling me with what was it, Bo? Not lust. Not then. Lightning, lightning as pure as the lightning outside that night. You're my lightning bolt. You like some people, love them even, but they don't make you tingle and jump. So I was going to marry a viscount who whipped my ass and left me in a puddle of my own pee, a viscount who'd never make me shudder, and I thought of you, who did, and wondered if you would still. And you do. Right now, in fact. What is that? This scholarly young woman who can hardly stand her own touch for various reasons we're trying to explore was going to marry this odious creep, this moneyed, titled odious creep, and what were you going to do, Bo? You didn't come to my rescue. So I married him, and then, and then you came.

You'd been sick, sick in body and soul, and you came to see if I was happy because it would make you happy. Is that it? Make your pain worthwhile? This Egyptologist whose arcane forte is how priests made colossi speak was living with Reinhard Heydrich because, what, because she couldn't think of anything better to do? No, she had plenty better to do. She needed to have her ass whipped because of what happened in Galilee. Yes! That's it, isn't it? The viscount was going to beat it all out of her and then she would live the rest of her life as if everything was all right. Aisling's thing needed to have her ass whipped, needed to stand in her cold pee and think what dreadful, what foul thing in her attracted Medea and her faery bun. Are we making progress, Bo? I was going to stand in my cold pee for the rest of my life in honor of Aisling.

Sally

You make me shudder, Sally. You didn't, Barbara didn't before, before Aisling's bedroom. No, wait, that's not true. You started to make me shudder when you flew into home plate, when I glimpsed your streaked panties, when you grinned at me, when I suspected you would always know what I'm thinking but might not hold it against me, might not pretend to be indignant at the dirty little boy. You were too honest a girl for that. You had no airs about you, no ploys. You weren't a

145

tricky girl. Do you think Aisling was? When you grinned that day I thought you might be my friend, and Barbara would never be, as much as she pleased me. She just wouldn't go that deep inside me—and yes, I know at this minute you'll be thinking of the barn window and me the bolt in you—you make me shudder, and you kept on making me shudder long after Galilee shut down and you'd gone home, all this time, until now. And every bad thing that happened to me I knew I deserved, like my mother almost scalping me with a bike chain, because Aisling saw something, knew something irredeemable in me. But then there was you, and I never saw anything in you that attracted harm, that inspired evil, and you liked me, you let me in you. Well, Aisling put me there, but then you let me, you wanted me, and I wanted you. Have I gone off track? Am I shedding any light? Maybe I should make some more drawings. Talk less, draw more. See if I don't have to lift the pencil off the paper, see if it all comes to me of a piece. I'll do that.

See this drawing of my mother lashing me with the bike chain. She's hot for Aisling. I know, I know, it has nothing to do with Aisling. But it does. She's beating me, she's tearing Aisling out of me. Did she know what Aisling did? I don't know. But I know that's what she's doing here. And next thing you know I'm bleeding out in the hot August sun, leaning against the garage in Woodstock, New York, bleeding out, blinded by my own blood, liking its taste, falling asleep, hoping never to wake, not to this nightmare, this mother, this hell. Then Lois from next door comes along. Lois is hot for my mother. My mother is hot for Lois. She poses for my mother, they play with each other. I'm hot for Lois. She tends to me. Drives me to the hospital, lies her head off to cover my mother's ass when the nurses ask how this terrible accident happened that leaves my scalp hanging loose. I listen to the lies like a movie. How interesting they are. How well Lois lies. The nurses are nuns. Are the nuns buying it? I guess they did, as I never did see any of those authorities. My mother takes off to the city. Let Lois clean up the mess, the boy, the blood, the story. I get better, I take off, I survive in the streets, I get drunk with merchant seamen and they get me a job on a banana ship as an ordinary (very ordinary) and the next time I ever see my mother is when she thinks she's swindling me out of Dominick's will. His will, which I never did understand, so why should I benefit from it? But my mother never knew me well enough to know I might think like that.

And by the way, you weren't standing in your cold pee, you left the fucker. And by the way some more, you had a home to go back to, I didn't, and I envied you, and was a little angry, too.

Bo

Dear Bo,

The question is how much light can we bear.

I'm not sure we remember all we told each other walking through the sea grass, tipsy on salt air and each other. Do you remember blurting out about Tessa peeing on you? She was bigger than you for a while and she ran you down over and over and peed on you. Well, that's quite a prologue to rape, isn't it? This boy-girl knocks you down, pulls her panties aside and pees on you. So what do you make of the world after that? I had no such preparation, but you had already been forewarned of darkness up ahead, and when it came you couldn't help thinking Aisling's daughter had softened you up for it, could you?

I can't go on. Your last lines devastate me. Tomorrow maybe. I can't imagine what you made of it, what you make of it now. I'm sorry.

Oh, did you and Lois....?

Sally

Lois. Yeah, I think it was the only way she figured she could keep me alive. I wasn't eating or talking.

Here's what I make of it, Sally.

Watching all the exhibitionists wanting to be watched, needing to be watched, is hard on the digestive system, they're so hurt, so incapable of digesting neglect. Even if they bump my table, spill coffee on me, make a show of parenting or greeting each other, I feel a certain embarrassment for them. They are like Tessa. I had to do something about her, I had to wait to grow a little, but in that predicament I understood my own sorrow, I understood her sorrow, even when we were too young to entertain it. Something had happened before this obscenity, something more obscene had befallen her, and when I dropped the cellar door on her head it wasn't to knock sense into her or even to hold her off, but to divert our attention from the strings that were pulling us. Much later when you were gone and we intended to make love we couldn't because we had looked down a black hole together and had seen the inhuman faces of our parents. Yeah, about that, after the war she came back from Arizona and looked me up. I felt so sorry for her, but I couldn't, and now that I think of it maybe it was okay because she could just write me off as weird or gay, and she's half right, I am weird.

Bo

I'm glad I wasn't the girl you had to conk on the head. I'm glad I was the mystery you wanted to solve. If you're weird I'm weirder and Tessa's weirder than that. But I'm sure something vital to your being was washed out of you, some essence essential to our survival washed away between Tessa's knees, something you'd already lost when Aisling called you to her bedroom, when she invented a reason to spank you and then tampered with you, making sure you'd be spacey on her fragrance, dazed in the company of her privates. That's why you can turn Tessa into poetry, and how you finally responded, because poetry, like your drawings, like my insights into far time, must be refined by dreadful fires. All the light we emit, if we emit light, comes from an *auto da fé*. Aisling is our *auto da fé*. We were burned at her stake. We died at her stake for her sake. What are we now, Bo?

Let me tell how it was for me.

Away, get it away,
get that thing away from me.
I must have it as much as it must have me,
get it away, and that's how my life will be—
stuck, clogged up, hurting there.
The words don't come, they're not there,
they're lost in a tunnel,
not that it was exquisite,
that moment left back there,
but that it didn't leave voluntarily—
we were torn away, thrown back
into a childhood blackened
by what happened, yes,
that's how to describe
that sexual orchestra conducted
by that witch-priestess,
that experiment where innocence
was sucked out of us.
No words come, just the music,
terrifying, dragging us
back there into that tunnel
where we can't breathe, where
we gasp, we die, we live
and can't get out to be here.

Can you draw it, Bo? Can you draw that? That what, I don't know? That scene? That incident? That evil? That ecstasy. Can you, can you please make more sense of it than I have? Can you draw light out of it? Did we ever really come back out of that tunnel, back down from Aisling's inlet? Can we live our lives not having come back? In the tunnel? Do we need each other to do it? Are we the only ones who can help each other? Is that why holding hands in the cordgrass comes to me each morning, because we're the only hands we have to

149

hold? Or can we just encounter it, ourselves, each other, here, for a while, and then go on separately? Can you draw it? Can you draw it out of Medea? I'm dying to know. We have been dying to know what happened, haven't we? Not the facts, not the photographs, so to speak, not the statements, depositions, etcetera, but what happened in our marrow, our blood, our circuits. What did we really make of it, and what did it make of us? Golems, globs of mud and ash? Zombies? Hashasheen? Or darlings, Bo. Could we be darlings? Whose darlings? We were darlings that moment at home plate, weren't we? Were we darlings in the window, in the cordgrass, in the tides, in half-sunk *Ludilon,* were we darlings then?

Sally

Darling. I've never called anyone darling, no one has ever called me darling. Here are my drawings. Here's Tessa. Don't fixate on her hand parting her panties. I know I drew that well. Look at her mouth. See. There's some kind of vindication there. I know, I know, ecstasy would be more plausible. But I see vindication. She needs to do this. She's almost drooling. Do you see it? It's as urgent to her head as it is to her bladder. Now look at Aisling. Same problem. Your eyes are drawn to my ass with her finger in it with me between her legs, like a pig at the trough. But look at her eyes. Remember them? They're wild, feral, triumphant. I'm faceless. I've lost my face in her crotch. She's pulling me towards her. Her? What is that, her crotch? Look at her eyes, her face, they're completely divorced from the work at hand, they're in another dimension. She is divine. I'm gone. Never existed. Never will. There's just fallen Aisling looking up to the heavens defiantly. Is this the moment, Sally, where we forgive her? This moment in this drawing? I have to hand other drawings of you and Aisling, me and you, the three of us. I don't want to play a game here or to gain control, but I'm afraid to send you these other drawings until we deal with this. You asked me if I could draw it? Yes. You asked if we could bear the light. Not sure. I know I'm withholding light by not sending the other drawings, trying to hold onto myself, trying to not sail off a shelf.

Please forgive me. If I couldn't draw Aisling and Tessa I'd be dead by now. My mother, the artist, the art teacher, she told me I had no talent for art, none. I know that's why I can't use color, not even pastels or chalk. But why can I draw? Whose gift is it? Who gave it to me? Her? None of my shipmates would ever forgive me for being gay, or a faggot, as they would say. But they pardon me for drawing, not because I make drawings of them, which they like, or of gulls and goonies, but because of the way I'm looking at them, as if they matter. They do. They matter. They don't know how I'm saving my life. Saving Aisling is incidental.

Bo

Forgive you what? Trying to stay alive? It's my ass, too, there between her knees, my ass with her finger in it. That's exactly what happened to me, too. There I am praying at her goddam altar, incense rising, bell ringing as the host is elevated, holy communion right in my little soaked face. Bo, I don't think we could ever have said these things without your drawings, not even us, not even two people who know more about each other than anybody else does or ever will. I understand perfectly your withholding the other drawings. I couldn't have dealt with that much, with so much. It would have made me angry. It would have been crushing. And you understood. We will always see our little wet faces in each other's faces, but perhaps in their translucence we'll eke out light.

I sat on the loo a few minutes ago trying to measure the distance between my ass and her crotch, or your ass and her crotch, because it seemed to me from your drawings that Aisling had a very long arm. But we were kids, nowhere near as tall as we are now, and she was a giantess, wasn't she? How tall do you think Aisling was? My guess is almost six feet. Or perhaps I've stretched her in my imagination. Remember those big straw hats she wore? In retrospect I think of Flora in Sandro Botticelli's *La Primavera*. Do I do Flora an injustice? Was Aisling as beautiful as that? Do you remember that she wore high heels, even in that bedroom, doing those things? That was no accident, was it? How old were we then, Bo? I can't remember, can you? I know I was a little fuzzy between the legs. I know you were fully capable of you know, poking me pretty hard, poking her. But how old were we? Surely there was no way we were ready for what happened, not even if it had happened just between us. But Aisling taught us, and we learned, better than we learned algebra. Didn't we? Were we up to algebra by then? Do you remember? Oh, Bo, I know, I know exactly what you're going to say, you're going to say, Sally, algebra means the joining in Arabic. Tell me you were going to say that, Bo. But remember that in Arabic it means the joining of the broken. Think of it, Bo! The joining of the broken. I do remember tutoring you, you were bad at maths. Was that later? But together we were algebraic, and together with Aisling, as you say, divine.

How the hell did you become a ship's captain? That requires trigonometry, doesn't it? Celestial navigation. Why didn't I know you could draw? I used to draw, remember? You're masterful. Not just good. How? How did we become what we are, whatever we are, crippled as we were, terrified? Me with my stammer, you, you with what? What were your damages, your impairments? Oh, I know you said in the Longboat, in the rain, that you were an unreliable sexual partner, so you live like a templar, celibate, not wanting to disappoint a woman, not wanting to disappoint yourself. But you didn't, did you? You didn't disappoint either one of us in the Longboat. And if you had, I would have improvised, I wouldn't have let you fail me or yourself, because we like each other, Bo, we trust each other, because we were forged in fire, Aisling's fire. We know what we're made of, and nobody else will ever quite understand. We don't quite understand, but we're trying, aren't we? Yes, we're Aisling's damages, and we're her salvages, or it it our salvages? Aisling the alembic and algebraist, Sally and Pip the concoctions, the tinctures.

A funny thing James Joyce wrote to Lucia, his daft daughter, not that he wasn't daft first. He said he didn't care if anybody understood *Finnegan's Wake* because all they really had to do was listen to its music. So maybe that's what we're doing. Listening to our music, which includes Aisling. Does it include Barbara, Tessa, any of the others? Are they, what, Greek chorus, Aisling's courtiers, palace guards, statuary? How are we to get them? Do they matter? I think so. Can the Ravishing Do-Gooder be understood without her hatchling? Can my panties be understood without Tessa's? And, speaking of Joyce, remember the more than 200 olfactory sensations in *Ulysses*? Well, what do we do about the olfactory sensations of Galilee? The bay, Wynant's Inlet, the barn, Aisling's bedroom, Aisling's inlets, me, you? I know I could be a bit ripe, and God knows Aisling could, but what about Barbara? And Tessa's rain on your face? Is this all fair game between us? Necessary? What must we remember, knowing we can never remember anything accurately? What can we make of what we've already made of what happened? All our lives since then we've known more about each other than we should know, more than anyone else knows or will ever know—how much more can we bear to know? And what to do about it? Will it help me understand how priests moved statues, or claimed to? We are each other's darkest secret. Will it help me in my career? Will it help you in yours? Will it distract us, divert us dangerously? Will it burn holes in us? Or will it light our way?

Sally

Look at this boy with his knickers down, Sally. Remember knickers? This isn't the way it happened, not exactly. It's allegorical. His hands are locked behind, concealing his little ass, but he's got something in his hand, his left hand, Sally. That's important. They forced us lefties to be right-handed in those days. He's got a pocketknife in his left hand. Never mind the rest of the picture at first. There's this boy in the foreground, his back turned to you. It's all about perspective, like a de Chirico painting. But that's a kind of pun. Whose perspective? The artist's? The viewer's? The boy's? He's looking at two doors, side by side. On the left is Aisling. She's looking out, straight at the boy. Her left shoulder is leaning against the doorframe as if she has just turned towards the boy. Her left hand is on her crotch, a familiar pose. But her right hand and forefinger are pointing at the boy. What did you do? her body language seems to ask. Because he did do something. Now look at the man in the right-hand doorway. He's looking while holding his cock in his hand. Oh my God, I can't believe this is happening to me, his body says. But what is happening to him?

It's Mr. Bradshaw, Sally. Remember him? He was a member of the cast of a famous radio show whose name I forget, if I ever knew. He condescended to come to Galilee to teach us. I don't remember any of his classes. I hated him. He was in charge of Saturday night baths. Not for you girls, I'm sure. That might have been Mrs. Lieberman at the time, right? Can you believe we bathed only once a week? He lectured me about the smegma that collected under my foreskin if I didn't wash properly. I could see it coming. But I wasn't sure what it was. His lecture seemed interminable. We uncircumcised gentiles have a special problem, he told me, because this foul cheesy stuff lurked under our foreskins. He started handling me. My knickers were down but not off. Then he invited me to handle him, this quivering candlestick with a big red knob at the end that glowed and smelled salty. Open your mouth, he said. I conveyed the idea that I ought to take my knickers off, which seemed to please him. But I was after the pocketknife in my pocket.

If I cut it off it won't bother you, will it, Mr. Bradshaw?

Can you believe little Pip said that, Sally? Can you believe any kid would say it? I was determined his cock was not going to be my lollipop. I don't remember seeing Mr. Bradshaw after that. I guess I just suppressed it. And I guess he decided little

Pip was a dangerous fucker best avoided. But in the moment that he waited for me to decide whether to enjoy the pleasures of his cock he looked up at the ceiling and rolled his eyes as if to say, Look what I have to put up with, Lord? This evil little boy is subjecting me to this disgraceful behavior. It was going to be evil little Pip's fault, Sally. Until evil little Pip pulled the knife and changed the game. That's what I learned to do at Galilee, change the game. It was a lot more valuable than *Silas Marner.*

That's why the boy here holds the knife in the hand he was taught not to favor. His trusted hand, the hand he trusted to warn that handsome prick that sometimes the difference between angels and demons is a hair. So there he is in the doorway lamenting to God for the indignity to which he has been subjected, and there's Aisling asking, What did you do? Because Pip certainly did something, and it's unlikely there was ever any discussion about it. And you know what, I should have made Aisling smirk, because she would have, wouldn't she?

But what of us, given this perspective? Is Mr. Bradshaw and smegma in any way responsible for delivering us unto Aisling? And why didn't the evil little Pip bring his knife to Aisling's party? Well, I think it's because the little demon enjoyed her scent a good deal more than Unctuous Bradshaw's, enjoyed everything about her a good deal more than he enjoyed anything about the put-upon Bradshaw. Enjoyed it, was crazed by it, dazed by it, dazzled by it, frightened by it—and God knows what else. God knows but has been too stingy to enlighten me.

So what are we by the time of our stunned, stupefied walks through the cordgrass? Revenants? Remnants? Remnants of our former selves and whatever those selves were becoming when they were interrupted by the Bradshaws and Wynants of the world? We don't know what we were becoming, so remnants of what? Revenants made of what?

I know this. I left the better part of any sexuality I would ever have, would ever offer, or share, in Galilee, like a discarded crab shell on the beach of what happened. Left it. Not lost it. I didn't lose anything. It was stolen. We were looted, plundered, savaged, and whatever we enjoyed, whatever we learned to like, well, that served to enhance our guilt, our shame. We saw right away that we had been chosen because of something dirty, soiled within us, and it never occurred to us that the kids we knew, the ones we liked, the ones we loathed, had also been chosen and looted and plundered. And if that had occurred to us, would it really have helped as much as shrinks seem to think? I don't know. That boy was willing to cut off that strutting cock, I'm sure of it. And that knowledge—I think you can see it in the boy's carriage—is going to be much more chilling to him than anything Aisling ever did. It's the reason Handsome left him alone. He knew the evil little shit was capable of amputating his problem. And the evil little shit would know it for the rest of his unnatural life.

So what kind of lives do revenants, the remnants, live? Are we pretenders? Do we pretend nothing happened, or are we writing back and forth here because we've decided not to pretend? And if anybody ever is damned, at what moment were we damned, Sally? When we consented to worship at Aisling's altar, as I didn't consent to worship at Handsome's? Did I merely bring a knife to the altar as others might bring a rosary?

At what moment did we walk out of a room as revenants? Whose revenants? A priest baptizes you and you forget him and he forgets you. A doctor delivers you and you probably never know each other. People save our lives and become faceless. I remember Handcock but not his face. But I remember so much about Aisling I hardly know where I put it all in my brain. I spend whole nights rummaging for memories of her, and while they may still excite they mostly sadden me. They fill me with dread and… mournfulness.

Aisling made my life a dirge. A mourning for the boy, for her, for you.

Bo

Dear Bo,

Okay, here goes. I'm going to try to make the colossus speak. It's just after dawn. The light has been pricking the blinds where they're stitched, so my room is filled with dots of light. I take this, as any Egyptologist might, as the moment when the sun pierces the tomb to where someone much too important in life lies attended by her shabtis. Are we Aisling's shabtis, Bo? You know what they are, right? The little statuettes that attend the great as they rest. Has Anubis been here? Last night? Here goes. This is my best understanding of Aisling, nowhere near as penetrating as your drawings, but perhaps less enigmatic. Ready, old chum? Here I come, panties flashing, here I come into your mitt, catcher. The third baseman is closing in behind. You're moving up in front of the plate. You're going to try to squeeze me out. He's optimistic because he's a newbie and doesn't know how fast I am. You do. You know I'm coming in flying, and I think—I'm grinning that grin—you'd rather crouch there hypnotized by what you see than tag me. Don't think I don't know that, prepubescent as I am. I know it. And the wind is favorable—

Every time will always be the perfect wrong time for the three of us. We are each other's short-circuitry. Whatever we intend to enjoy, to celebrate, to feel, will short out and smell like burning wire the minute our minds, like children's fingers, find their way to the wrong place, the dank place, the pungent place no one else inhabits. We three are inviolable, having so much known each other that all we really know about anyone else is that they're not Aisling, they're not Sally, they're not Pip, and so, God help us, they're not, not at all. We are each other's adytum, each other's inner sanctum, and it can't be drawn without us as loci.

I've said it. I've said it to lovers. This is the wrong time. But I've never said it's always going to be, not until now. It doesn't matter if I'm saying this to a tape recorder, or a shrink, or a confessor, or a ghostwriter, or you. It doesn't matter. The words will hang in the air like ink, just as the acts hang in the dripping caverns of my mind. Not because they're immortal. Not because they're well said. Not even because they should be said. But because this kind of profanity is ineradicable. We'll have to live a thousand lives to expunge it, and even then we won't be illuminati, we'll be their shabtis, serving them in their necropolises, those colossi. But wait. What if Aisling—and the other betrayers, the other caretakers and guardians who tampered and tinkered with us, what if they're priests, not colossi? Well, if that's so, were they moving us to speak? What did we say to them in our silences, Pip—now Bo?

This can't be rubbed out like a masturbatory itch or a sob or a death wish. It can't be laid to rest or put to the test. You are the way you're electrified.

Okay, here's Aisling. Speak, Aisling!

There's no telling why I smile or why it's inappropriate. At funerals when someone is trying to be serious, whenever someone is trying to be serious, I smirk. But one thing's certain about my smile, it's not inviting you in, where you might think "in" is. This particular kind of death serves me well in Arizona, where all of us are sun-blind to the interiors of our souls. "Rest." Curious word. There is no rest for us, me, Sally, Pip. I took care of that. Maybe I meant test and only thought I meant rest. Maybe I meant both.

Am I writing this down? Am I talking it into a gizmo? Am I telling it to a shrink? It doesn't matter. It's written on the walls of my mind. It's my *Mene, mene, tekel upharsin.* If I start wandering into rooms and forget why, if I start forgetting where I put things, I won't forget this, I won't forget them. They're the murals in the Sahara, they're the words on the walls of my skull. And I know that naked me is painted on the interior walls of their heads, too. Nobody has ever been as naked. I've never been as naked. And if you stumble on this because it's in a novel or a poem or some scrapped diary don't think for a moment that I thought you could absolve me of one damned thing. You can't, even if you wanted to.

Sally and Pip are my sand dunes. I know how and where they drift. I can identify their every grain. I am their Tuareg mistress. They're my unfortunate slaves. But how unfortunate? What did we exchange more precious than our body fluids? What if it wasn't evil so much as circumstance? What if we weren't predator and prey so much as hierophant and adepts? Yeah, I know that sounds like defense, excuse, but what if that's actually how our lives played out? What if that's what this is about, this facile chit-chat that may yet cost us what's left?

Hear her, Bo, you hear Aisling speak? Okay, that's all I get right now, all I can imagine Aisling saying. I'm into her. More than you, Bo. Yes, yes, I know I watched you plumb her, in her dressing room mirror. All three of us watched. I know. But it's not what I mean. I'm into her. I get her, or at least I get an Aisling I can work with. She too needs to make the stone colossi speak. She too needs to know their secrets. Maybe there'll be more. I don't know. But I hear her. Right now I hear her.

Sally

Dear Sally,

I get it. I hear her. I hear the colossus. We'll never get her out of us, will we? And now I know she can't get us out of her. But here's what I want to ask: How much can we share with each other, Sally? I saw you and misread the situation. I was leaving. Everything's all right, I told myself. You were all right. But I was really afraid of you, afraid of what you might have become, somebody who belongs, somebody normal while me, I'm still crazy, dirty, dumb. Were you afraid of me? You just shared more than we shared then. I mean, being hot for each other, scared, unstrung, what's that compared to all the secrets we've pulled around us since then? You can make colossi speak. I can draw. And we've both read enough poets to imitate some of them. And if we share drawings, incantations, invocations, what's left at the end? Do we shake hands and say goodbye? Do we kiss each other on the cheek? Do we just sign off? Will we always own half of each other and go on crippled but unable to bear each other up? I left because I didn't want to ruin what we had and I was scared of what you might have become, how you might have come to hate it, hate what we did, what was done. But I don't want to be scared of you, Sally. I don't want to be scared of Aisling.

I live in a world where I can get away with drawing. I make pictures of shipmates and give them away. I can be forgiven for that. They can forgive me because I'm a good sailor and have a few ribbons to show for it. But they wouldn't forgive me a poem. That would make me queer. Queer the way we're queer, Sally, not the way they'd mean it, but the way we know it. Queer as hell. My mother the artist, do you remember her? Big floppy straw hats, looking like a Gainsborough. Well, she was a terrific colorist, so I could never use color. Do you understand that? Good luck with that. I don't. And the poems, well, they're how I figure things out. Kind of like trigonometry for navigation. I figured it out because I needed to. Not to please that fucking Mr. Curry—remember him?—he told us we'd probably flunk if we didn't instantly get the algebraic bafflegab he didn't know how to explain to us. They're how I get from one place to another, and there be dragons in between. Here, I'll show you what I mean:

I remember being old, I remember being young,
I remember something else all my life, nothing
to do with time, but rather a gleeful imperative
to let you and this and that fall on me like rain,
to slip between the drops, to be at the center
when they collide, to enjoy the privileges of light
and to remember that nothing being done to me

defines me long enough to matter. I remember
being something other than my circumstances.
Occasionally I remember being you before
you had to account for me. It hurt and yet
I think it is the reason that finally we met.

I call this one "Cross-dissolve." I don't know what to call
the other one.

Too big too loud too bright too close,
you-it-they closing, and then
fading in & fading out of faces,
cross-dissolve & punishment,
the lure & hopelessness
of having anything to do with them again
other than haunting each other
in a moldy grange
and getting hit by taxicabs
or run down by pickup trucks
or dying in an antiseptic place
too big too loud too bright too close
to ward off the inevitability
of losing another piece of mind,
a piece not necessarily at fault,
perhaps a patch or glue that held
something together that now waits
for the right moment to come apart
to be a part of some other thing
perhaps a monster made of parts
of my life so sickening, so sharp
I can't think of them without bleeding.
Yes, I could bleed out, depending
where I sit down or fall,
good reason not to trust euphoria.

About the time azaleas yelp
I forgot how to tie my shoes.
It was a summoning I took
for erasure, a wiping out of me.

I stood on 116th Street in May
unable to tie a simple bow.
Butler Library shilly-shallied,
commitment to hold shape
wavered. Was I who I said I am?
I fished the 19-year-old
I squatted in for a name.
He did not rise to the bait.
I thought the subway imperative,
but where should it go,
Yeshiva up or down to the sea?
My mind had blown out
information I didn't need,
or if I needed it, for what,
to suffer more indignities?
Are you okay, I asked?
Who are you? the squatter said.
Not okay, let's go to work.
But which of my four jobs?
Funny that, I knew I had them,
but I could remember only one.
Didn't know it then, but it would be
the best job I'd ever have,
selling newspapers on 8th Avenue.
Didn't need name, could make
some kind of knot, greet
hundreds of anonymous friends.
What a job, to hell with Columbia,
to hell with me, but what then,
what if at one a.m. I had nowhere
to sleep? I must live somewhere
beyond these knotted shoes.
Maybe the pigeons would tell me.
I sat in Bryant Park, faithless,
not a boy, not a man, nobody
but a being tipsy with glee.
It couldn't last, things to do,

places to go, but not the books
I left on a bench in the azaleas.
They could tell me nothing,
not even Spinoza could figure this out.
Dawn came up, clink, clink, clink
data came back to me, but not
the same, tampered with, tinkered,
unwilling to prove itself,
be interrogated, suspect, and yet
all I had to go with, to be me,
all there was beside fried eggs,
burnt coffee, indigestible toast.
No wonder the azaleas yelped,
I would too if I'd been asked
to perform under the circumstances,
and yet perform I did, and when
Herbie Goldberg said Goonite Pip,
at least I knew my name, assuming
it wasn't Goonite. Herbie knew
this Dostoyevskian fool, thought
well of him, it seems. So all I had to do
was to sit still, or maybe seek
a compromise, something between
the drunken glee of namelessness,
the ecstasy of being data-free,
and having a case for my brief
(a box for my grief?), a compromise
between what I'd been and spectral this
which now rolled out like a blue carpet
for wedding guests at Saint Bartholomew's.

Amnesia, for all its side effects,
is aphrodisiac, but you've got to be
a bit sardonic, both jaded and innocent
to enjoy it, and who is that?
I stuffed it in my yellow suitcase,
that cardboard box in which I arrived

163

at boarding school when I was five,
the box in which I left when
my mother kicked me out
on my 18th birthday, left to find
how clever amnesia is, like hide-and-seek
with a well-loved girl, genius
roving your lobes in mufti, a spy
you may occasionally arrest
and waterboard, learning nothing,
an entertaining, frightening spy
you finally marry, come to trust
and even depend on her betrayals.
What do you think of that?
You'll never know, but you do know
how she came to your rescue if not why:
she came so you wouldn't implode,
so the big black hole within you
wouldn't suck you out of this universe.
Yes, you might have gone to another one,
you may be in another one, for all we know
of celestial mechanics and their works,
for all we know how we emulate them
in our frenzies, you might have gone
to pieces spitting out memories
bigger than refrigerators, but amnesia
has been kind enough to choose,
redact, to constrain your impulse
to be gone not as in woebegone
but as in free to mix with elements
that guarantee you nothing
but cosmic lust, not even result,
but ennoblement beyond understanding.

To writhe in transport
is not a commercial issue
but an algebraic reset,
a rejoining of the self

to primeval substance,
restoration of order
in this rapine world.
That's what these kids
salvaged from their ruin,
what they wrote in silence
in the air, their writ.
Nothing auto-erotic
or neurotic—a failsafe
to let them start again,
let them meet again,
try again, fail again
and finally to triumph
over orchestration
and choreography
juicing up the melody.
Nothing in their victimhood
should lead us to suggest
their brokenness was not remade,
in their original images
so that no one can bear
to look at them who doesn't want
to see what's truly there.
To learn where their eyes might rest,
to learn to remove themselves,
they had to trick the scales
by which we measure success,
and that required tincture
of speechlessness, sputter
that turned to stutter in Sally,
a smile turned to deadliness
in him, but first they held hands
in salt marshes and longed
to turn what they had learned
so bitterly to what they yearned
out from under Aisling's hand.
Neither my head that needed

to be examined nor my nethers
fit in that cardboard box,
that ominous yellow suitcase
with its green and red stripes.

Get out by 8:15 a.m.
and have your head examined,
said my mother's loopy note
written on unlined yellow paper.
It's only in your head, she always said,
and all my sanity resided in this:
Where else, I asked myself?
Not because I knew the answer
but because I thought my head would do
for starters and more profane places
could be sorted out if I lived that long.

I wasn't a plucky little drunk,
but something of the cock-eyed sailor
was getting up steam in me.
Why, specifically, 8:15? Don't go there,
it's a trap, like all her utterances,
but where, where should I go?
I didn't belong as joiners fit
dovetails into grooves
or as masons shake each other's hands
or in any sense of the word acceptance,
but I caught wicked fastballs
and wielded a mean hockey stick,
I threw runners out and most of all
I liked the sea, settledness
that others called turbulence.
I understood its long game,
the utter meaninglessness of 8:15 a.m.

Okay, now you got it, right? That's what I mean. Something
I'm not sure I could say straight out in a letter, something that has
to be run through the Enigma Machine and enciphered by ghouls
with silver lightning runes on their black collars. Something

incredibly sharp young women figure out in Bletchley Park. Young women like you. I have to hide behind the code because I don't want to reveal the troop movements of my mind.

Bo

Utter nonsense, Bo. That's not why you make these poems at all. They're not your Enigma Machine. That's intellectual sloth, what half-assed critics say when they don't have the wit or will to dive deep, when they're jealous. The poems are another kind of light. They're not how-to manuals, they're not textbooks, they're about their own business, and it doesn't matter whether they're ever published, just as it doesn't matter whether the drawings are exhibited or ever rendered into color or ever made into paintings. They exist. We're sharing them. We talk about something that was done to us, something Aisling did to us. Okay, that's one way to think about it. But what we share, what we know happened in Galilee between us, that's ours, our treasure as well as our hurt, our damage. And we are the only two people on earth who can fondle it, who can move the stars in their courses, affect the tides, restore order to the cosmos, fingering each other's memories. No therapist, no other lover, no interrogator, no interlocutor can do this. And this is something you knew, you apprehended and came looking for me. Something I didn't know and now do. This came out of your drawings, your poems. Hold onto this, Bo. You don't do color because you can't bear it any more than I can bear touch. But it's not lost on you, it's lost to you.

You remember I told you when I awake I see us in the high grass, hand in hand, stunned, crazy, not in love, but in a trance, entranced? It's not a dream. I'm sitting here at my desk feathering my muff, something she'd love to see, something she did see. I smell her, Bo. And I know if I aired out this room I'd still smell her. She drifted in through the blinds. These pinpricks of light get behind my eyelids, they sting my brain. Morning after morning I sit here seeing two children walking hand in hand in a fen. It's important not to say they're us, Bo. Just two children. The dawn is behind them, behind, the watcher and them. They're looking out on Great South Bay. The sun's angle is wrong for this, as they would be looking south and the sun would be rising to their left over Montauk. But this is the way it is in this not-dream, this artifact of a dream, this recurrence, these hieroglyphs. I'm supposed to wake up this way, considering the children. The girl's towhead is ablaze. The boy's long brown hair is teasing hers. He stands to her right, so the wind is to his right. All this is important. I don't know why. I'm not sure how old they are. But the girl is beginning to be shapely. I can't get out in front of them. I'm trying. I'm running. I'm out of breath. Is it Sally? Is it Pip? Me and Pip, that is? It must be. They must be. I'm not sure. I'm not sure they're quite human. I think they might have been sent, sent to Wynant's Inlet to tell me something after all these years. I don't know when I started seeing them, started conjuring them. Or are they conjuring me? I'm not going to see their faces. I know that now. I think it possible they're dead, in the way Pip and I died back then, back there. I think they may be walking towards *Ludilon*. I think they're about to sail away. Perhaps they can't until I let them go. But I'm not detaining them, am I? Yes. I am. That's what I know this morning. They need to go. They need to sail *Ludilon* away. I'm detaining them. I'm not one of them, and yet I am.

And here's Aisling again, Bo.

Our fingers always find their way to the open socket. Every important moment shorts out, smells like burnt wire. We're the ruins of flash fires, gutted. Our breaths gutter our hopes, our good intentions. We should wear condemned notices. We're dangerous to inhabit. We know so much about each other, we know how dangerous it is to know anyone well. We only thought we left that stifling room. The war goes on overhead, underneath. I can't come up from the evil depths. Can Sally? Can Pip? We can't be rid of each other or ourselves. We are each other's sockets in lamps we shouldn't have stuck our fingers in.

I ran away to Canada with Rafe because I couldn't take another goddam minute of my parents' Mary Baker Eddy. I mean, she was all right. I liked *Science & Health*, but all that Congregationalist sanctimony latched up with it…. They had a righteous answer for everything, even scarlet fever, and being right only made me hate them more. The war came and Rafe, beautiful, dumb Rafe, joined the RCAF. The Battle of Britain came and a Messerschmitt 109 shot him down, and I came back to Galilee tumescent with Tess, grieving and aggrieved. Nah, pissed is the right word. And now Galilee was full of Norwich kids evacuated because the Krauts were bombing the shit out of their homes and schools. And I wondered how many of them were like me, so angry at their parents they couldn't talk straight. And there was Sally Beaumont and her older sister Barbara, ravishing as Vivian Leigh, prim as a Puritan, Sally with her helmet of white-blonde hair, her sloe-green eyes, Sally, all legs and a kind of fixity that scared the other kids. And there was Pip Didschus, the only American kid, a kid with a suspiciously German name, except he was only half German. His other half, his father, his unknown father, was Arab. He wore his mother's name. But he was the kind of kid who wouldn't, couldn't wear any name well. And Sally wasn't born to belong anywhere either. I wanted something out of her, still do. Something I can only describe as *this*. Whatever *this* means Sally had it. She was whatever she was—urgently, immediately, unquestionably. She'd never be anything else, and I had this compulsion to eat her. Pip, even across my knee, even when I had complete power over him, even when I scared him, scared me. I knew he was deadly in a way I'd never be, in a way Spitfires and Stukas weren't. And I wanted that deadliness. Whatever bullshit you fed him, whatever lie you told him, he'd swallow it for only a little while. He wouldn't wake up in the morning your fool, and that seemed precious and unattainable to me. I wanted a husband, a lover like him, and I was furious with him, still am, because he wasn't old enough to take, so I took him anyway, took him as he was. That's what the damned war taught me, the joke it taught me. And I took Sally too. And I married them. Wouldn't it be funny if they ever got together again, if they did marry? They could hate me together. But what else would they do to me together? Fuck me? Eat me? Love me, even?

I've lived all this time feeding on you, Pip, knowing I stand in every other woman's way of knowing you, pleasing you, having you. You're my wealth, my secret treasure, my mojo. I own everything you couldn't become because of me. Everything you became. I took it. You can never have it back, but if you read this, if it gets to you, you can hold it to your nose and smell it, like the panties I held up to you. You won't smile. You never did. Your green stare will shade your face. The green-eyed two of you, can you beat that, you two green-eyed devils. It's like the green Renaissance artists applied to flesh. It underlies your appearance. I remember, as you remember the taste of my sweat, my twitchy nipples which I painted for you and Sally with my more profane excrescences. You live in that room. The three of us do. It's not demolished in our heads. The Victrola is still playing, its needle still scratching, Bing still crooning, the goddam Chattanooga Choo-Choo still chugging on Track 29.

Nothing has ever happened since. Everything has only seemed to happen, gotten in the way back, like the illusion of marriage and all that claptrap. We died. I know you will know what I mean. Listen to the damned fools talk about sin. Sin? It that what it was when the abyss looked back? A great black hole that swallowed us, leaving our facsimiles to confuse the hounds, to be imposters. Were the hounds confused? Did we trick the inquisitors? Did they get secrets out of us? What did we become?

My detective tells me you're a decorated sailor and now you're a Merchant Marine captain. I know you're still the boy supplicating between my knees, kneeling not as much in terror as in prayer. Every cup, every chalice, every glass, every spoon reminds you of me. I am everything you can't contain. That's glory, but it ain't alleluia. Can you imagine how beholden I am to you? I set out to be your god, and you said yes. I know. I know you couldn't say no, and that's my crime. But was it a crime or our revenge on the circumstances that made you orphans, made me a rosy riveter and a foolish widow? You could have ruined it, and you didn't. What did I ruin for you? Your life? You were my sacrifice. I cut out your heart at the top of a temple. I made it rain. I stole your fire, and it has burned in me ever since. All that purity belongs to me, not you. You refined me. I coarsened you. Do you hate my name? The Wynant is gone, but not for you. What else do you hate? I'm dying to know. You're taller than me now, you weren't then, you weren't finished growing. You were feverish that first time. Scarlet fever. You ran out barefoot in the snow, in your tatty pajamas. You dived head first into a snowbank and barely made it back to your room, you were shivering so hard. Mary Baker Eddy didn't help you, but I did. I made you warm again. You climbed down a drainpipe from the fourth floor, the top of the old grange that we called Galilee. Some haven. How did you get back up to your room? And then I found you feverish and shivering in that closet of a room across from my apartment, and I took you to bed, drunk as I was, and stuck my titties in your mouth. Do you think of that? Of course you do.

That's what I hear Aisling say, Bo.

Sally

Dear Bo,

I'm in the outré theory business, Bo. You get that, right? I think it was no accident you and I got into the navigation business. Egyptology isn't all about reading hieroglyphs, you know. It's about finding things, and that means you have to know why the Egyptians put things where they put them, why they faced things in certain directions, why they calculated where sunlight and moonlight would strike at certain hours. You, of course, go hither and yon by the stars. You, I imagine, depend on certitudes. I do when I can find them, but Egyptology is riddled with uncertainty, best guesses, hunches, solutions that sound persuasive from the lectern but prove foolish in the field. Here's my hunch about us.

I think Aisling's magnetism was so godawfully powerful it swung our compasses permanently. Is that the word, Bo, swung? I think when we looked out over Great South Bay from the back of Galilee we thought we were looking north, so of course north, the front of Galilee on Sunrise Highway, was our south. I think we left Galilee swung around inside ourselves. Our heads would have had to figure it all out, but our emotions were always looking out to a north star that wasn't there. I think we've never gotten far enough away from that magnet to align our compasses. I think what we think is normal is us mimicking behavior we saw in a movie that struck as what normal people do in certain situations. I used to go receptions at Cambridge, not to meet people but to figure out how to act, and I'm sure I picked some calamitous models, prigs, pricks, twits, prats, wankers—I thought they were smoothies. Did you do that? No, you didn't, did you? You just felt more, stared harder. I loved that in you. You never thought you had to fill a vacuum. How did you get that way so early? Everybody would be yammering and I'd look at your hands, so perfectly still at your side. And you always seemed to be looking into my eyes, no matter what anybody was saying or doing. Why did you do that, Bo? It never disconcerted me. I always felt that was just about all I knew about normal, Bo sharing a joke with me, silently. But that was after Aisling messed with us, wasn't it? After she began messing with us, I mean.

When I write to you, if I don't finish the letter in one sitting, I have a hard time picking it up and going on. This sob balloons in my chest and I can't rub it out. I remember you gazing at people like Bradshaw and Lieberman and them getting all twitchy. I remember Eleanor Wynant telling you it's not polite to stare. And I remember you staring at her and her fingering her brooch. I always wanted to laugh, and I always had the sense that you knew I did.

So what do you think about my compass idea?

Sally

Dear Sally,

Magnets are the death of compasses. Sometimes even after you swing a compass—swing it back to order—it won't work right, it resumes its wrong position.

I hate exhibitionists. I want to kill them. When some loudmouth comes into a room I just want to kill him. They mean to skew your compass. That's what they do. Ulrike was like that. You die and she steals the attention at your funeral. You get married and all eyes are on her. But she didn't do it like Aisling, and I think we have to consider that. Aisling wasn't a talker. But she radiated heat. She made your lights flicker. You sensed her a mile off. I knew when she was coming to my room long before she came. I'd be sitting at my desk in West Islip Public School and I knew there'd be Aisling that night. I had this feeling that when the curtains moved or the shade shook Aisling was about to spring something scary. I could hear her think, but not in words. I could hear thoughts forming in her head before they were words. And I think—tell me if this is so, Sally—that she reckoned that was what was going on between you and me. I think maybe that's why she put us together. We fit, and she knew it. There was a lot more to Aisling than Rafe would ever find out, wasn't there? And she knew it.

Her despair was rooted in knowing it. Maybe there was even a part of her that didn't want him to return, didn't believe he would. And, who knows, maybe a part of him let himself be shot down because he knew he didn't fit, he didn't suit Aisling. She was a witch and all he got is that he didn't get it, couldn't get it. So what would there be between him and Aisling when he came home? Tessa? Aisling skewed Rafe's compass, Sally. He was all catawampus when that Messerschmitt got him in its crosshairs. So we're trying to get out of her crosshairs, aren't we? And maybe the only way to do that is for us Messerschmitts to get her Spitfire in our sites. There's a military term that supply officers use, surplus to our needs. The Navy sells off its surplus. I think Rafe was surplus to Aisling's needs. Are we?

Bo

Yes, Bo, yes! I'd see her considering me, like a Rotterdam diamond cutter figuring out just where to strike the uncut stone. I wasn't exactly scared. I was thrilled, but not like the expectation of ice cream or going ice-skating on McKee's Pond, not like that. Something beyond me, something I hadn't felt before. Not like Nosferatu's shadow on the wall, either, but something going haywire in my circuitry. I think—this is a wild guess—she was more scared of us than we were of her. What the hell are these faery kids doing here? she wondered. What can I get out of them? What can I put in them? How dangerous are they? Who put them in my path? Who put her in our paths?

Sally

Dear Sally,
Sometimes my memory is as cool, spare and exacting as Edward Hopper—the hard-edged shops of Babylon. Sometimes my memory is as fluid as Renoir—my first kiss, from Mary Corbett of Copiague on the Merrick. Sometimes my memories are cubist or surreal. But I think Aisling in Arizona or wherever the hell she is, hell maybe, answered you. I think she heard the priest and spoke. I recognize her. That's the Aisling I never could have described but always knew. I think a bolt of sunlight struck her where she lies and she heard you. I hear her. Not you. Sometimes my memory is like Seurat or Manet, changing as I move this way or that way or away, but not the Aisling I see and hear in your letter.

She wanted to eat us, and then we'd be her body and her blood. And I think she did. It's no good, no damned good at all to call her a child molester, a rapist, a predator. It's cheap, unholy. It's beneath us. It was a communion, a mass, unholy, unnatural, ineradicable, and if we do nothing else together, say nothing else, at least we've come together again to that understanding. Who are we to forgive? Who are we to absolve? Who are we to understand? We've conjured her, we've raised her from the dead, we've raised ourselves. We've… I'm scared shitless. I don't know how you did it, but you're sure as hell not an Egyptologist for nothing. The colossus has spoken, God help us. The bell has rung, the mass has begun.

Bo

Dear Bo,

It has been 152 days since you wrote. Are you safe? Has Aisling silenced you? Will I hear from you again? Did I somehow go too far? How far is that? The bell rang, did you run out the door into the sunlight, into a storm? I don't like being out on this limb. But we've both been out on a limb since, since what? Galilee. Since then. Both left staring out of that barn window into a storm. Both left holding hands staring out into Great South Bay, not looking for U-boats, as we used to do, perhaps not looking at all. Perhaps blind, stunned by the light. After that everything was too big, too bright, too close, too loud, too smelly, wasn't it? But we're not to each other, are we? Still not, not then, not now. Why is that? Shouldn't we be each other's bane? I'm scared too. Are you going to let me be scared alone?

Sally

Shouldn't Aisling be our bane, Sally?

No, we're not those things to each other. Yes, you stunned me into silence. I'm okay. At sea. My home. I was waiting for a funny thought, something inappropriate, impertinent, as Eleanor, Aisling's mother, often used to say. You and I were impertinent. Remember? Was that before or after, you know? I've been waiting for something impertinent to come to mind. I've been waiting for dignified Eleanor to call me impertinent, so that I'd know I'm still alive. But I know I'm not. I know I'm the walking dead. This is what I do when I can't decide. A gig breaks loose and beats itself against the hull of my ship: I know what to do. A fire breaks out, somebody gets hurt: I know what to do. I have to hurt somebody: I know what to do. When I don't know what to do, something's up, something serious, not like the life and death shit I usually have to deal with, but something that's deep-down sick and painful. I wait for a word, the dumber, the crazier, the better. And here it is, 152 days late, or later. It's love, Sally. Love. It's the only way we can get to Aisling, to understand her, just a little. Otherwise we're sketching and conjuring and summoning a villain, a demon, and what good does that do us? What light will that shed? When someone's serious, I don't smirk.

Here's how I got to it, and it's as deep-down unsettling as every other damned thing about it, about what happened. I'm five years old. September. Piles of maple leaves burning on a cinder driveway. I've just turned five. I'm standing in the driveway at Galilee. Remember that cinder driveway? It was an oval, one entrance at the Babylon side, the other at the Bayshore side. Ulrike, my mother, is standing there in a pleated white skirt and a big broad-brimmed straw hat with a blue ribbon. White pumps. I remember every damned detail. Aisling is standing in front of us assuring my mother, not me, that everything is going to be all right. Everything, that's what the little Pip Dipshit was supposed to believe, and he didn't believe a word of it. And he might as well not have been standing there at all, Sally, because these two beauties are hot for each other. Really hot, flushed. And little Pip Dipshit gets it. He's not supposed to get it. They're not supposed to get it. But they're getting each other, all right, and he knows that he's not only irrelevant but he's also in for it, whatever it is, whatever it turns out to be, it will get him.

Now remember, you two are already at the school, you and Barbara, and I've never lived with this hot beauty who's being assured she's doing the right thing, never. She swept in and took me from my grandma, and Peggy, my nanny, and Aunt Dorothy, swept in like a tropical storm and swept me off to fucking Galilee and Aisling. And here they are, simmering on pinkish cinders, pretending it's all for my own good, when all they really want to do is something with each other. So love is the key, Sally, to get past the cinders, the smoky do-gooders, the situation. That's as far as I've gotten. Love between us? Us loving Aisling? Us loving the ravishing do-gooders who sentenced us to Galilee? I don't know. But they can't be stick figures for our convenience, even if we were for them, because then we're just their goddamned shabtis. I've been reading Wallis Budge. We have to love our way through to what we don't know. Or put it this way, we have to raise *Ludilon*, refit her and get the hell out of there. Sail her from Galilee to the Dead Sea, from Mark to Matthew, John to Luke? Yeah, that'd be the day. Then what? Damned if I know.

Bo

Forgive ourselves, Bo? Is that what you're talking about, Bo? For what? Christian forgiveness? Was there any in that Calvinist hell? Okay, where to begin? Suffer The Little Children To Come Unto Me. Remember that banner in our Sunday school? Just who suffered us? Who suffered us to come unto Aisling's bun? Who is suffering us now?

Whenever someone asks where to start, someone else says at the beginning. Where is the beginning? She's angry. There's the war. We were evacuated, we Brits. You were dumped. Aisling loses a husband she hardly knew. As handsome as she's beautiful. The war fucks everything up, everyone. So, thinking of Occam's razor, the simplest reason Aisling ruins us is her life got ruined, so why shouldn't ours? But she wasn't as mindless as that. She's angry. And you and I are the most impertinent kids, maybe even the savviest. So why not us? Scotland Yard might go with that theory, just to close a case. But I'm thinking a Venn diagram is better than Occam for this. You take three interlocking circles and you put sets, what they have in common, in each of them. And you see where those sets end up, what they have in common with each other, and if you're lucky you end up with one set that survives all the questions. So what's the biggest question? Is it why Aisling ruined us or is it whether she ruined us? And what you said about love, maybe that's where love comes in. Were we just objects, dolls, dildos to rub against, or were we collaborators in a project that now, finally, not then, we're capable of understanding? So in one set she's an evil bitch who ruined us. But what if we were recruits, volunteers even? What if she recruited us to settle the world down, to steady the stars in their courses, to restore order, to take something back from chaos. What if we were like Vikings enslaved by the Saracens on the North Sea and taken back to the Barbary Coast where eventually we're offered freedom if we convert to Islam, which happens to mean submission, Bo? What if we're shaped, not ruined? What if the trauma that makes us hyper-vigilant, that wakes us in the middle of the night, is also our salvation? What if she is the scent that haunts us, the taste that quickens us when otherwise we'd sleep and be found in our sleep and carried away? What if that's our ability to make the colossi speak, to summon out of the illusion we call time? What if a goddess toyed with us and enjoyed it so much she endowed us with certain gifts?

So then what's this? Frottage? Are we just rubbing against each other for warmth, for surcease? Are we just rubbing our memories together to start a little campfire before going our separate ways?

Can you take it, Bo? Is this bearable? Do we have to loathe her? I've always had to struggle to loathe her, because I think I should, but I still feel her tongue on my clit, her fingers in me. And so do you. Who are we if we loathe that? But on the other hand—here's another set—how the hell do we share this knowledge, assuming you and I agree on it, with anyone else, with anyone who didn't stare into those brown eyes with their yellow spears and know that nothing would ever be the same? Her eyes, our abyss? Who's going to love us, or even like us, once we reveal how sick we are, how altered, how ruined, how seared, how blessed? Can I get away with that word, blessed? Is that the next set, our blessings from that ruinous girl? She was a girl. I know, you're going to mention Tessa, who was our age, who ran you down and peed on you, Tessa, Aisling's creature. And we don't know what happened to her, before or after, do we? All you know is she was odious to you. Later, when you went to back to Galilee with her and as a young man, well, if it had been me, or Barbara, or Dolores even, you could have, you would have fucked one of us. But you couldn't fuck Tessa and you blamed yourself. You wrote yourself off as impotent, because you couldn't rise to the occasion, couldn't overcome your memories, couldn't imagine Aisling's daughter as Aisling.

You had a perfectly natural reaction. You called it sick and tragic. What if it had been me, Bo? We would have gone to Aisling's old apartment or the barn and we would have done what we did, and then God knows what, and we have no idea what would have happened, do we? But I was gone, back to England, and you wrote me off, and I wrote you off, for the sake of convenience, until you got injured and lay in a hospital bed telling yourself you had to see if I was all right. All right, or was it my panties you wanted to see at home plate again, my indecent grin? We didn't write each other off, and I doubt Aisling wrote us off. She's as stuck with us as we're stuck with her.

And was everything fucked, everything and everyone? Mightn't we have done a pretty good job at that without the war? Remember this, Aisling was smart, but how smart was it to marry dumb-ass Rafe because he was so good-looking? Maybe she would have fucked up her life without Hitler's help. And maybe we would have been fucked up in different ways, just by different people.

Send me a drawing. Or two. Draw this, Bo. Help me, help us. Draw a Venn diagram, anything. Help me.

Sally

Bo,

As you haven't written back, and I don't know if you will, I'm pressing on, which is what I think both of us do in our own ways. I read once that sailors say certain ships at flank speed have the bone in their teeth. Do you? Is that you, Bo?

Nothing has ever been so exciting. It's important to say that. That's the trouble with harm. There have been times when I haven't even been sure it was evil.

As for the men in my life, well, all I know for sure is that none of them have been Pip.

And all the women, more or less, have been Aisling.

I've never been able to talk about it or even write it out. I'm not afraid I won't wake up—perhaps I'm afraid I will. Wake up, that is, without telling this story, if it's only to myself. It's the story that keeps erasing my image in the mirror, and I guess I'm worried it's going to hang around when I'm gone, and I'll be remembered by its odor. Or somebody else will look in that mirror and see me, the me I couldn't see.

Here's what happened last night. I put my glasses behind a pillow—I wear reading glasses, Bo—and it might as well have been a mountain on the eighth continent, because when I woke up I didn't reach for them, like I always do. It wasn't me waking up. It wasn't the person from whom you were 152 days away. It wasn't the daft Egyptologist with the great legs the wrong people are always getting hot for. It was this person who saw thoughts hanging in the air before they decide what to become. Incipient thoughts, maybe an incipient person. I stood barefoot looking out over Great South Bay, like I always do, but you had gone away, 153 days away. I was afraid the person in the mirror would be an old crone, me chatting with a granddaughter in a garden. It would be winter. I'd be wearing a gray-blue watch coat and she'd be bringing me dead flowers. Or, more likely, there'd be no one in the mirror. But whatever I was going to see, I didn't need those glasses.

My ghostly eyes, so not like Barbara's dark blue eyes, were busy seeing what no one else could see, thoughts playing with themselves, undecided what to be. Oh, and one other thing, I hope this doesn't scare you, I was mad at you for not being there so I could tell you all about it, just as I'm doing now. Are you there, Bo? Wherever there is?

I've gotten in the habit of dying. It's like you and me fucking each other silly, scared to death, panicky really, and not knowing if we were having fun or dying. I've never happened on anyone to tell me. It's like watching myself from the ceiling or through a keyhole or sitting in a café and watching myself through a steamy window. I start talking to myself as if I have a friend. I keep asking myself how I'm doing and what I think. How're you doing, Sally? Sally grins. I think and when I think I stink, I'd answer, and then I'd give myself a loony grin, just like when I jerk my panties till I come. I know it's crazy as hell, but what difference does it make to a dead girl? You're not supposed to tell a man these things. You're not supposed to tell anyone these things. Not supposed to have these thoughts, use these words. Not supposed. I certainly don't have that kind of relationship with Barbara. Any chance of that died when she glommed onto the fact something was up between you and me.

I like zombie movies because I understand them. Vampires are hopeless optimists. There's nobody to tell any of this to, except you of course, and crazy Sally, you know, the one I'm not. And I'm probably driving you off, babbling like this, but you're the chance I have to take. I'm the chance you took. And we sure as hell took our chances with each other when we didn't understand what the hell was going on. Probably we still don't, do you think? I die in odd places, peeing in the dark, all eyes, fucking somebody I hardly recognize, talking to my mother, especially talking to her. It's my only out, talking to her, dying, sort of like the vanishing Cheshire cat. She thought I was her luggage, which of course she lost whenever possible. She never could explain me to customs. I never could explain myself. I keep dreaming about her body parts on rainy tar-papered roofs. I get off on thinking about beating her. I don't want to leave my dead body with her. It may be the only reason I got married, so I'd have somewhere else to be buried. But my dead body was everywhere I'd been, hanging around in grotesque positions.

Whenever someone asks where to start someone else says at the beginning, but I'm not sure what the beginning is. If it's a pop quiz I'd say that barn window was the beginning. There we were, two impertinent improbables. You loved Dolores. What did you feel for Barbara? Did you hanker for Barbara but love Dolores in some pure, hopeless way? What did you feel for Barbara? For that matter, what did Barbara feel for you? She seemed all grown up to me, but she was only two years older. Now she seems like a child. Did I ever tell you what I thought about Dolores? I thought she was the kind of girl and would be the kind of woman who'd disappear when you touch her. And all there'd be is that enigmatic smile, those painted tin cups filled with imaginary tea, and you in that gazebo waiting eternally for the girl who never was. That's what I thought. And then there was gritty me, daftly athletic me, not quite as fast as your ghost-girl but a much better all-around athlete. You liked me, you trusted me, and after that moment at home plate I knew you'd think of me at night when you shouldn't. On the other hand, the left hand, why shouldn't you have? It didn't matter if Dolores and Barbara were forbidden, because I wasn't. Not that I was loose, or anything like that, and not that you were ready for anything like that, but because something about me got to something new about you. And I knew it. I knew it and I liked it. My eyes were scary where Dolores's eyes were cornflower-sweet. Her hair sat politely on her head; mine was so fine a sigh stirred it. I would do, wouldn't I? Did you know (this is a pun) English is the only Germanic language with the verb to do? Do you know that?

But here's something else, Bo. Girls, girls like Adrienne—remember her?—were always talking about getting over on boys, toying with them, and I hadn't thought about any of that stuff at all, but I liked you, I just liked you, and I wouldn't have hurt you for the world. And I think maybe that was the most important thing you knew about me, maybe even the reason you came to find me. I don't know if Barbara would have played with you, hurt you. But I do know she had a sense of ownership where you were concerned, and she never forgave me for whatever happened, whatever she still doesn't know. Dolores? I can't say. And for some reason I don't want to know how she turned out, perhaps because, while I have no regret about taking you from Barbara, I didn't want to hurt her, and I know I did. I know you did. Tell me in your next letter, assuming I hear from you again, whether you're wondering if Aisling interfered—isn't that the quaintest word in this context?—with them. What could we do about that if we knew? What could we think? How could we situate such knowledge in our brains? How could we bear it? How does Aisling bear it? Eleanor? We have to assume Eleanor at some level knew, don't we? Maybe not my mother, busy in Norwich dodging bombers and my father's chums? Or maybe not. But maybe your mother, Ulrike, maybe she knew. Not maybe. Probably, and probably resented the hell out of you for knowing Aisling in ways she didn't. Or did she?

Barbara always wants to know where my head is. Is it sisterly to ask? She's a good sister. She tried to look after me. I'm sure you thought her too old for you. What was it, a year or so? But I know you remember her fondly. You're proper, like her. I'm not. I think it was your proper demeanor and the way she stroked your arm without saying anything that bonded her to you. I loved that. It's why I'd never tell her what happened between you, me and Aisling. Never. She was your workmate, I was your playmate. You did dishes and laundry together. We were, the three of us, sexually awakening. I know she was more aware in that respect than you and I were. You know how I know, so I won't go into that. Sometimes I imagine Barbara and me sitting white-haired in a rose garden in pewter blue overcoats talking about all this. It's snowing lightly. It has to be snowing. But I don't want to be silent that long, so I'm telling it to you. Besides, it would hurt Barbara as much then as it would now. I have to hear myself saying these words. I have to consider my inflections. Without this act of recollection there is no peace, and there may be none with it. Barbara liked you and you liked Barbara in a way that is out of my reach. I understand. And I understood you and Dolores. We all did. The earth would have tumbled from its orbit without you and Dolores in that gazebo. So many of us savored that. It was important to us that this fey vignette be repeated over and over. Otherwise something we didn't want to happen would happen. But it was different between you and Barbara. You were as forbidden to each other as you longed for each other, and I don't know why, I never will, and I'm not sure I want to. And if I see you again, if we see each other, I don't know what to do about Barbara, what to tell her, what not to tell her. What to hide, what she would want me to hide, and I've noticed, of course I would notice, that you haven't asked about her. Well, she's married to this perfectly marvelous research physician with whom she grows more impatient as time goes by. She told me once he was a friend and a fond lover, so what the nature of her impatience is I don't know. But I know this, she doesn't touch his arm as they pass, and I know that's all that kept you sane and alive at times in Galilee. Shall we talk about that? Dare we? My relationship with her, my friendship, is too important to splinter or shatter, and so is yours even though you haven't seen her all these years. So we must be careful, mustn't we? Tell me how to be careful, Bo, careful of our friend Barbara.

Sally

Sally,

Ludilon appeared adrift in an inlet after the Great Atlantic Hurricane of September 1944. You and I swam out to her and found her anchor rode flopping against her starboard prow. The bitter end looked as if it had exploded. We climbed her stern ladder and found hemp line in her lazarette. The table was set in her salon, plates and flatware jammed up against the table's fiddles. We found a knife in a drawer and went forward to tie the hemp line to her samson post. Then we jumped overboard and hauled *Ludilon* to shore. It was hard work. She was a seagoing lapstrake trawler, about forty-two feet long. The tide was coming in and nudged her wave by wave up onto the beach, which was littered with all kinds of flotsam. We were flotsam, you and me. Hurricane flotsam. I had an inchoate feeling that *Ludilon* was my life. I had found my life, her table set. We knew a little about boats, Galilee being two miles east of Babylon, where there was a big commercial fishing fleet, so we found a brass seacock and opened it, draining the *Ludilon* cabin, bilges and lockers. Then we shut her seacock with a sledgehammer we fished out of a gear locker. The obvious questions—what happened to her crew, how she got here—came to mind, but we refused to discuss them because now *Ludilon* was ours. The Great Atlantic Hurricane, that killer storm, had brought her to us. Only many years later, long after you and I had been pulled apart—in more ways than one—it occurred to me that *Ludilon* had no homeport painted under her white-lettered name, outlined in black. How could that be? Was she in transit to a new owner? Yeah, but her varnished stern revealed no evidence of a previous name or homeport. I like the mystery far more than the plausible answers.

Ludilon is my healing stone, my nav star, my true north. She makes ordeals endurable. She is my only home. Other homes are encampments, posts, way stations, bus stops, airports. I shared her, share her with two people only, Dolores, whom I loved as a child loves, and with you whom I didn't know I loved. I'm, I think I'm too sad to go on just now, to finish this letter. I just realized that Dolores was hurt in ways I can't imagine once it happened, this pivot, this linchpin we are talking about. This catalyst. I was no longer her friend, *Ludilon* was no longer her home, her hope. Did we in our terror and ecstasy murder the Barbara and the Dolores we knew? Are they war casualties as surely as we are? She disappeared. We saw her every day, but she was gone, vanished. I kept on having tea with her in the ruined gazebo, but everything was as ruined as we were. You kept your distance, reverently, but I was aware of you watching, keeping your distance, and so was she. There was something going on between us in everyone's peripheral vision, and I think it pained us as much as it did them. I'm so sorry, so very sorry, Dolores.

And I know you are, Sally. And we do address each other at great distances, like this, don't we, although we'd never admit it for fear of being seen as loonier than we are. And we do hear each other, and deny it, don't we? I have to stop. I have to go play music for the dolphins at the bow. I have to make them happy. They like Mozart.

I dreamed about *Ludilon* last night. Ghosting a dry streambed in a dark empty city made of blood-red bricks. I dreamed of running in sunny suburban streets about seven feet in the air, just out of Aisling's reach. Not always Aisling. Sometimes my Uncle Norman, who smells like skunk cabbage. I dream of getting *Ludilon* underway in a blinding snowstorm. Dolores is on deck and I have to clamber up the gunwale after pushing *Ludilon* out into the inlet. I like snow melting on Dolores' eyelashes. That's what I think of when my malaria comes back and I'm burning up: Dolores' snowy eyelashes.

Why must good come to us at others' expense? Why must others' sorrow underlie our happiness? Is it so for whales, for dolphins? I can't come back from the sea to such a world, such a mean world. I'm used to scanning horizons, an eighteen-mile expanse of peace. Most of the time. Why is the light that shows us a way forward strewn with the wounded and dead? Why does what we're doing, Sally, come at the expense of knowing who we hurt? And if we could override that hurt, that knowing, what kind of creatures would we be?

It's no use making love, no use even trying. Nobody else is you, and in this new light, this talk, I'm not sure you will ever be the Sally in the barn window, Sally in the Longboat, Sally on Clare Bridge. I'm not sure of me except when I'm a sea creature. Yeah, yeah, I know, what if someone somehow reminds me of Aisling? Or you? That's a different story. Depends on the time of day. Depends on where. Depends on how mean I am at that moment, how disposed to use someone for some end, some mean, cold, dead end. Depends on scent, perfume, mold, sweat, color, sound. Sound. Aisling whispered. So that's a turn-on. Depends on, oh God, let me try again. You know the actress Susan Sarandon? Wonderful actress. Love her when my head's screwed on straight. But it usually isn't, which is what this is all about, and then, at those times, I can't bear to look at her. I can't bear to look at that beautiful face because it's too damned much like Aisling's face. You get the drift, right? Not that I do. Remember her in *Pretty Baby?* I could've killed myself the night I saw that movie. Could've? Hell, should've, is what I thought for a long time. I could kill myself now, remembering what we, you and I, Aisling's children, her instruments, did to Dolores and Barbara. And there are no amends. No healing. We'll never know exactly what we did. They'll never say. But everything changed, grew dark, cold, strange.

Ludilon is all, everything I ever read, every prayer I ever said, every dream and recognition, every memory—cargo in her hold, and now it comes to me after a lifetime overlooking it that she had no homeport, none. You swam round her, climbed her stern ladder. I remember *Ludilon* in white letters outlined with black, arching slightly across her bowed stern. Because of *Ludilon* I became a sailor. In her honor, by her command. My life's her logbook. But it was also because I somehow betrayed Dolores. She was meant to sail with me, not you. But she would have been less capable, less willing. I knew that, too.

I never wanted to hurt anybody or anything. But sometimes I'm not sure that served me well. Wait a minute. It's not true. I did once want to hurt somebody. Billy, that bully, my roommate. He pushed me around. He stole things from me. He threatened me. And one day I went to the closet where we kept our baseball gear and I got my ashwood bat and walked through the hallways looking for him. I passed through the pantry. I remember what you said: Kill him. That changed everything, Sally. Before Aisling, it did. Barbara stared at you. She was stunned. Like a Viking shield maiden, you said: Kill him. Everybody, even bigger kids, got out of my way. I saw through the fog of rage. And when I found Billy for just a second he came at me, and then he cowered and ran. I ran after him. I hit him I don't know how many times, at least once on the head. I don't think he ever looked at me again. But I looked at him. A lot. And everything changed. I changed. Later I saw a drawing of a Viking, sword in hand, stalking the hall of a church in England or maybe Ireland, and I remembered that blind walk through the halls of Galilee looking for Billy. I never again saw the Vikings as looters, pillagers and rapists. I saw instead myself looking for Billy Kilgore with blood in my eye. Nobody was going to stop that boy any more than a priest or Saxon warrior was going to stop that Viking marauder, and even when further abuse and worse came my way I remembered that Viking and I lived to be him again. I would be that Viking, *Ludilon* my dragon ship.

In some ways this is my rutter. A rutter is a kind of log sailors kept before there were charts. It described what the sailors saw so that others could use what they had seen to sail the same routes. We saw a mermaid glowing off a spur of land to our port side. There were sirens calling to us from a heap of rocks just outside the harbor at Carthago. And so on. Then, when sailors began to make charts, they used rutter notes to mark certain places. Here be dragons, for example. I sure as hell knew where the dragons were. And the sirens, too. So yeah, consider this a rutter. I'm tempted to invite you to follow me into hell, but is that what it was? Perilous, yeah. Agonizing, harrowing, wounding, crippling, all those things. But not without their delights, their raptures. I don't want to paint a dark picture. I want to paint an accurate picture. I mean, if you want to follow somebody's rutter you'll want to bring something back from Calicat, Cathay and The Japons, something costly, something somebody besides yourself might want, might pay you for. You're a kind of merchant. It doesn't matter what you're trading in. It could be pearls, emeralds or epiphanies. It could be souls. It could be your past lives. This is my rutter. Pip's rutter. I know damned well there are charts, and they'll steer you well, but they won't steer you where Pip's Rutter will. They're too official, too authoritative, too pretentious. You can't buy this rutter.

Ludilon was there in the inlet just east of Galilee when I got scarlet fever. The practitioner came to read *Science & Health* to me, but what I thought I needed was a cool hand. I would have even settled for Tessa peeing on me.

Never occurred to me she was peeing on other kids. Maybe I thought I was special. Maybe I was just worried about the next damned thing that was going to happen. But incinerating in my sweaty bed next to the scary attic I would have settled for her to put out the greater fire. And then I made a plan. I listened to the snow piling up on the roof and pelting the windows and I made a plan. If I ran across the common area between our rooms, between Aisling's room and my room and the three Patterson brothers' room, I could get into the southside bathroom, the one that faced Great South Bay. I could climb out the window and slide down the drainpipe and run like hell through the snow to *Ludilon*, and everything would be okay. How it would be okay I didn't know. Maybe just sitting in the salon, with the table set, and… and dying. That would be okay. It would mean no more Billy, no more Tessa, no more Aisling. That it would mean no more Dolores, or no more you and Barbara didn't come to mind.

Who do we trust?

Certainly not ourselves.

I don't know. I don't know what I don't have charts for, what I can't figure out by the stars. But as I read your last letter I see that I have to make something more of Tessa, and I think you knew that when you asked what if I had gone back to Galilee as a teenager with you or Barbara or Dolores, not Tessa. What if it had been your idea? Well, with you it's a rhetorical question, isn't it, because how would we have resisted going back to that barn window? Isn't it the one thing we knew how to do very well at that age? I was still learning math, literature, whatever. I was still catching baseballs. But no lightning ever flashed at just *that* moment, did it? And we would have wanted to know if it would again. Is that something we'll always want to know? Is that Aisling's gift to us? She taught us how. Maybe we would have bungled into it, maybe not. But we weren't just sharing each other, we were sharing Aisling. *Do this in remembrance of me. This is my body, this is my blood.* Yeah, I know, we were Christian Scientists, we didn't go in for that Catholic stuff, but we know the words, the ritual, don't we? I remember the blood on your thigh, your golden thigh. I'm not likely to ever forget it. Was it a high mass, a holy communion, a wedding? Could you have been the blood, me the body, Aisling the priest? Here's a poem where I'm trying to make sense of Tessa. I have to call her Aisling's daughter. When I call her Tessa Wynant nothing happens. That disturbs me. She's not Aisling's creature, we're not Aisling's creatures. But she tried to make us her creatures, didn't she?

Bo

Dear Bo,

I can never tell where you are. The postmarks are merely where you've been. But I have a dire inkling this is the end of our string. You're not going to write again. You're not coming to Cambridge or Norwich to find me again. You've scared yourself. I've scared myself. We've told each other too much, said too much, revealed too much, and we can't live with it. Were we doing okay before you came to that lecture and then tried to walk out without talking to me? Was that okay, what you do best? Is that happening again? Will it always happen? I have a solemn resolve. I'm coming to New York. I'm going to ring your doorbell. I will sit on your steps day after day if I have to, until you come home from the sea and we continue this holy communion, because we were damaged and we were looted, but we were also wed and gifted, and nobody will understand this, nor should they have to. But how am I to explain to any lover when *that* moment comes that it's not his moment or her moment or even entirely my moment, it's Sally's and Pip's. And Aisling's. Who wants to hear that, except maybe us? So clear the decks, man your battle stations, I'm coming to see God knows what, to find out how we can go on. Can you bear it? Can you get your bearings? I'm sliding into your home plate again, Pip.

Yes, I always knew it was Dolores who was supposed to have been your mate on *Ludilon*. What kind of twit would I be if I hadn't known that? Your teas with her in the gazebo were locally famous. It was a foregone conclusion you would be each other's mate. The war might end, but somehow you two wouldn't. It was one of Galilee's most enshrined givens, and don't think for a minute Aisling and Tessa didn't know that, that it wasn't part of their calculus. But it wasn't part of mine. I didn't think Dolores was for you long before I thought I might be. I wasn't that kind of girl, I'm not that kind of woman. I liked you two in the gazebo. I liked the given imprimatur of it. And when I knew my existence had interfered, interrupted, I was as upset as you are now, realizing how often good comes to us at others' expense, at the expense of the very last people we wished to hurt. I too saw Dolores on *Ludilon's* deck. I too saw you both heading out by Fire Island into the future, away from hell. But then you saw me flying at home plate, and that wasn't either of our faults, was it? It wasn't your fault you loved what you saw, nor mine for my dirty grin.

But as I go aerial, dirty grin and all, as I leave third base in the wake of my pigtails, as I catch a glimpse of you behind your faceplate in Manhattan, I wonder—if we loiter in that barn window for the rest of our lives, lit up and electrified, will we ever be able to say when or if we grew up?

Sally

A message from the author

If you have enjoyed this book, my publisher
and I would be grateful if you'd leave a short
review at *goodreads.com* and/or at the website
where you bought this book.

Books by Djelloul Marbrook

Poetry:

- *Far from Algiers* (2008, Kent State University Press, winner of the 2007 Stan and Tom Wick Poetry Prize and the 2010 International Book Award in Poetry)
- *Brushstrokes and Glances* (2010, Deerbrook Editions, Maine)
- *Brash Ice* (2014, Leaky Boot Press, UK)
- *Shadow of the Heron* (2016, Coda Crab Books – out of print)
- *Riding Thermals to Winter Grounds* (2017, Leaky Boot Press)
- *Air Tea with Dolores* (2017, Leaky Boot Press)
- *Nothing True Has a Name* (2018, Leaky Boot Press)
- *Even Now the Embers* (2018, Leaky Boot Press)
- *Other Risks Include* (2018, Leaky Boot Press)
- *The Seas Are Dolphins' Tears* (2018, Leaky Boot Press)
- *Singing in the O of Not* (2019, Leaky Boot Press)
- *The Loneliness of Shape* (2019, Leaky Boot Press)

Poetry & Fiction:

- *Suffer the Children* (2019, Leaky Boot Press)

Fiction:

- *Alice Miller's Room* (1999, OnlineOriginals.com, UK; reprinted as title story in *Making Room: Baltimore Stories,* 2017, Leaky Boot Press)
- *Artemisia's Wolf* (2011, Prakash Books, India; reprinted as title story in *A Warding Circle: New York Stories,* 2017, Leaky Boot Press)
- *Saraceno* (2012, Bliss Plot Press, NY)

- *Mean Bastards Making Nice* (2014, Leaky Boot Press)
- *A Warding Circle: New York Stories* (2017, Leaky Boot Press)
- *Making Room: Baltimore Stories* (2017, Leaky Boot Press)
- *Light Piercing Water* trilogy (2018, Leaky Boot Press)
    I *Guest Boy*
    II *Crowds of One*
    III *The Gold Factory*